PROMOTIONAL MARKETING

Ideas & Techniques
for
Success in Sales Promotion

William A. Robinson
&
Christine Hauri

NTC Business Books
NTC a division of *NTC Publishing Group* • Lincolnwood, Illinois USA

Library of Congress Cataloging-in-Publication Data

Robinson, William A.
    Promotional marketing : ideas and techniques for success in sales
  promotion / William A. Robinson and Christine Hauri
        p.   cm.
    Includes index.
    ISBN 0-8442-3150-9
    1. Sales promotion.   I. Hauri, Christine.   II. Title.
  HF5438.5.R63   1991
  658.8'2--dc20

90-20955
CIP

Published by NTC Business Books, a division of NTC Publishing Group
4255 Touhy Avenue , Lincolnwood, (Chicago), Illinois 60646-1975, U.S.A.
©1991 by NTC Publishing Group. All rights reserved.

1 2 3 4 5 6 7 8 9 VP 9 8 7 6 5 4 3 2 1

Contents

Foreword

It was a day of paradoxes.

The relative comfort of the pristine corporate waiting room stood in stark contrast to the raw January day outside. My partner and I were about to make our third (and most important) presentation on a great promotion program to the Vice President of Marketing of a major consumer products company. This was the "deal maker" meeting.

With the presentation at last at hand, Arlene and I moved quickly through the usual amenities. The VP's lieutenants were our allies by now, so a few moments focusing on the VP was time well (if impatiently) spent. Kids, families, and respective football teams were all fine, but the weather provided a fine diversion. The ice had been particularly nasty that morning.

Finally, *the idea*!

Careful background working, meticulous preparation, and sizzling creative were layered with seamless acumen. But our trump card was a thorough approach to implementation and administration. It was a "can't-turn-it-down" deal.

In fact, we were already talking about how carefully we had considered all of the potential problems when it happened. I was starting to wax eloquent about the slippage problem when the VP interrupted.

"You know, slippage really *is* a problem," he explained intently. "Just this morning I nearly slipped on the ice as I was coming into the building."

The salesman's nightmare hit me; I didn't have a comeback!

While I was talking about a liability of hundreds of thousands of dollars in unclaimed prizes, my client's boss was worried about his bruised posterior.

How fitting.

The players (and companies) in this vignette are left anonymous less to protect the corporate ego than point out that such ignorance about promotion marketing at senior levels is not one company's problem. It is the greater paradox, and a compelling reason why, in today's business environment, this book takes on heightened significance.

As the Executive Director of the Promotion Marketing Association of America, I continue to uncover a notable lack of knowledge about promotion marketing at several levels. The various components of promotion marketing (sales promotion, trade deals, incentive programs, etc.) account for the largest discretionary expenditures in the marketing mix. Yet formal training for this discipline is virtually non-existent. There are no degrees in promotion marketing, not even a minor designation. A few forward-thinking schools like Northwestern University and the University of Texas at Austin offer "emphasis" programs, but even these have trouble maintaining focus.

Internal training programs at company level vary widely. Procter & Gamble's program, for example, is considered state-of-the-art by many for its thoroughness and precision. Unfortunately, the requirement that you must be a P&G employee to take advantage of it remains in place.

Smaller companies typically have neither the resources nor the dedication to match this commitment—which is ironic, since most no doubt share the same enthusiasm for sales and volume.

So the best source for industry information remains the open market place. It is here that Bill Robinson's works have for years excelled at combining solid business aptitude with a marvelous knack for simple communication. This book, in particular, provides that, but also adds an important and long overdue perspective on the evolution of promotional marketing to its current place atop the marketing mix.

Good promotion planning and execution is difficult and meticulous work. Yet Mr. Robinson always found a way to define his explanations in *usable terms*.

That is the highest compliment I can pay any communicator, and it is also a mandate for required reading for a certain Vice President of Marketing.

> Christopher J. Sutherland
> Executive Director
> Promotion Marketing Association of America

P.S. With some fast footwork about the "metaphor" to which we are sure the VP was alluding, we eventually got that deal.

Introduction

No one grows up wanting to be in sales promotion. An astronaut, a lawyer, a teacher, a crazy advertising creative, maybe a cowboy are all acceptable dreams for a youngster. But a career in sales promotion just doesn't carry the same excitement.

Yet here we are, all grown up, with some of the marketing community's best talent dedicated to the bottom line, in sales promotion. We all seemed to have come up through different avenues. Some started in sales, others in retailing, others in brand management. I started by selling displays back in the 1950s after the Korean War. We were art salesmen who started selling ideas along with the art—ideas like sales events, and gifts for retailers that were part of the display.

I've been in this business for more than 35 years and the ideas and artwork I've seen have taken on magnificent proportions. It has become a very legitimate, creative and important profession that none of us display salesmen of the '50s would have forecast.

Sales promotion as an industry seemed to take off on the same course as those of us in the business—no one ever planned on its success. For years sales promotion meant MDF funds (Market Development Funds, an innocuous word for slush money to pay off retailers for promoting your product), giant displays and tacky potholders.

But now the industry has grown up. And corporate offices want to see where those MDF funds are going and know that those costly displays can pay their way and move substantial incremental product. Marketers are looking to promotion professionals to build their brand's sales today to insure a future for the brand tomorrow.

This book is the story of how sales promotion grew up. We look at numbers and see that 1989's marketing expenditures put 25% against consumer promotion; 44% against trade promotion and 31% against media advertising. This follows an ongoing trend we've been seeing since the late 70s, (19% consumer promotion, 39% trade, and 42% advertising in 1976) and shows clearly that promotion is capturing a higher slot on marketers' agendas than ever before.

An equally enlightening conclusion that can be drawn from this data is that promotion held no place in the marketing totem pole as *there is no data* from before the late 1970s. While researching this book, we consistently found that companies had reels and cassettes, film and copies of ads and commercials. But hardly anyone kept promotional displays or ads, sales aids or sell sheets. Reasons—or excuses—for not preserving samples were varied. "We moved and didn't have room for displays." "Sales saves that stuff." (Wrong. They thought marketing saved it!) "What promotional material?" etc. We can conclude from this that promotion materials were simply considered less important than other marketing samples.

We found, too, that over the years promotion may have been the responsibility of any number of areas—from sales to advertising to brand management to marketing services departments to actual promotion departments. That was yesterday. The most consistent message we are hearing in today's maturing marketplaces is a new interest in what promotion *is* and what it should be doing for business.

As we chronicle the rise in importance of the promotion business over the past four decades, we also celebrate the events and people who helped bring it to the forefront. We've chosen not to name names throughout the years, only because we know we would miss so many of the important ones. But if you've helped raise the level of professionalism and interest in the promotion industry, you know who you are, and we applaud you.

How to Use This Book

This isn't a problem-solving book or a textbook. It is a book to be read for enjoyment, ideas, and trends.

Enjoy—I guarantee some of the examples from the past will bring back a memory or two, or at least spark a smile. Did we really wear bell-bottomed pants and drive cars with fins?

Ideas—I doubt if anyone can read this book and not be struck by *déjà vu*. So many of the individual promotions, situations, and solutions from the past arise frequently in today's marketing world. While technology and experience has led to considerable advances in execution, many of the past successes may offer just the right core idea to solve a promotion problem you have today. If you're looking for ideas, review the sample sections with an open mind, looking for applications to a problem at hand.

Trends—Think of promotion as being a raft in the ocean and U.S. economic conditions being the tides or waves. You'll see how major economic swells resulted in increases in promotional spending and often the development of new promotion media. You'll also see how smooth and even times led to a promotion status quo. The trends we see in sales promotion are the same as those that have affected other marketing functions over the years. By studying and assessing them, we are in a stronger position to lead the industry in the future.

Many Thanks

A retrospective on the growth of the promotion business cannot come to fruition without some very sincere thanks. The two men that inspired me to this venture were Howard Haas, formerly chairman and CEO of Sealy, Inc. and a lifelong friend. Howard suggested I share my remembrances of the business as a way to inspire others into this exciting field. My second source of inspiration was the first writer on the book and my oldest and favorite boyhood friend, Joe Sanders. Joe spent over two years of his spare time learning my business and philosophy while starting this book. Unfortunately, Joe passed away suddenly and never saw the book come to life. I know he would have enjoyed reading it!

Many business and personal friends have been involved and I hope to thank them all personally. My public thanks go to Essie Landsman, for getting the project started; MaryAnn Hay, for ongoing scheduling and administrative support; Casimir Psujek, Anne Knudsen and the other patient folks at NTC Publishing Group; Robin Levy Goldstein for research; the Ketchum Communications group for administrative support; Jennifer DeMille for editing; and Chris Hauri for picking up where Joe Sanders left off to finish this book on one of her favorite topics—sales promotion.

Here's to all of us in the business, near the business, or just redeeming coupons! Hope you enjoy this!

Bill Robinson

CHAPTER ONE

The Fifties: Cashing in on the Affluent Society

What a decade of opportunities! What a change from the war-focused forties! This was the decade of prosperity, when the pent-up demand for cars, televisions, and labor-saving appliances met head-on with the discovery of motivational consumer behavior and "brand image." It was the era when Detroit led us to suburbia and the need for "new," when television opened up the world to show us opportunities. . . . then told us we should all live as "Father Knows Best." "What's good for General Motors is good for America," announced Charles E. Wilson President of GM in 1956, and marketers from all industries and business were quick to tell us what else was good for us.

Americans returned from the Korean War to experience the strongest economy they had ever seen. Here was a labor force of veterans coming home to find jobs in the manufacturing of *consumer* products—televisions, washing machines, clothes, and cars—built not for war but for peace. Where natural resources and assembly lines had been dedicated to building planes and tanks for the war effort, they were now retooled to manufacture appliances and build homes.

Simple economics explains the fifties. During World War II and the Korean War, there were no consumer goods to buy. Once peacetime came, soldiers came back to work, start families, make their homes, and buy things. Finally, there was the supply necessary to meet the demand. And there was a labor force and natural resources to offer that supply and to fuel that demand.

Anytime there were inklings of recession, as in 1954 and 1958, big business reminded America that it was patriotic to buy. And it was marketing and communications that were driving us to buy like no other generation.

Two Cars in Every Garage

While America has always had a love affair with cars, Detroit's heyday was in the '50s. It was the automotive marketers that led us into "psychological obsolescence," making us think that "newer is better" so we traded in our cars every two years for the latest models. Each year the models got longer and lower until finally, when Directors of the Board complained about having their hats knocked off when entering the newest models, Detroit abandoned the height and length game and went after multiple purchase.

Automotive stylists were watched even more closely than fashion designers, as September heralded the unveilings of new cars. Across the country, these were the special events of the day. No one needed a chance to win or a rebate as an incentive to visit the auto dealers. It was excitement enough to see the new twin tail fins styled after the air force's twin-tailed fighter planes. Or to see the car that "America designed—the Edsel."

By the late '50s, if you weren't buying a new car this year, maybe you were entering the world of the two car families . . . a second car was becoming an essential for the new suburban families, especially if there were teenagers at home! We believed what TV commercials said when we heard, "The family with two cars gets twice as many chores completed so there's more leisure to enjoy *together!*"

What Made Us Buy

Coinciding with this surge for new things came Dr. Earnest Dichter with his "discovery" of motivational research. His recommendations to "sell the sizzle and not the steak" led us into fantasy benefits, often created through extravagant consumer research. "To women, don't sell shoes, sell lovely feet."

While Dichter's thinking led us to living out fantasies in public in our Maidenform bras, adman David Ogilvy brought us snobbery and "brand image." What began with the eye-patched debonair "Man in the Hathaway Shirt" took us into the image-laden world of today, where the label is more important than the ingredients.

It was in the '50s that Marlboro changed from a women's red-tipped cigarette into a "Man's cigarette that women like, too." All this was done with the help of a tatooed cowboy's hand that led to the single-focused Marlboro Man that followed. A 1956 Marlboro promotion even offered free hand tatoos— "transfer pictures"—to help drive home the advertising!

Enter, Mass Media

As the auto was moving us to suburbia and appliances were letting Mom have more "coffee klatch" time, television was moving into our homes. Had all these factors not hit at the same time, we very well would have had a very different America in the '50s and beyond. Missing television alone, we would never have been so impressed with Detroit, as the television commercials and coverage built the excitement beyond earthly proportions. And without television we would not have been able to *see* why we needed so many new household products. Without modern conveniences, we would not have had the time to enjoy ourselves in our cars, in our backyards, in front of our televisions. Most importantly, we would not have had the views of our world that television brought.

While we saw life across the oceans every night on the evening news, while we laughed at Lucy and Red Skelton, it was the television commercials that showed us the good life. Suddenly millions of Americans at once could see the trappings of the rich, the status symbols to strive for. There were accepted norms with Mom being a homemaker (a welcome relief for many after working during the war), cute well-dressed children, and Dad leaving for work every morning in a business suit.

On television you could see the latest refrigerators, pop-up toasters, food mixers and washers. And you could see how people you identified with or aspired to be like dressed and spent their leisure time.

We made our heroes overnight—like Joe McCarthy, Elvis Presley, and Charles Van Doren, winner on the quiz show "Twenty-One" and later found out to have been prompted to build the ratings. We moved our lives to our televisions with the advent of TV dinners, TV trays, and TV rooms. But this was early, still the golden age of television when we were still fascinated with what we could see. And how we could live. And what we could buy.

Facts from the Fifties

- GNP jumped from $300 billion to $400 billion between 1950 and 1955.
- 31 million families owned cars in 1951.
- Nylons dropped to 89¢ a pair in 1951.

EXHIBIT 1.1 In the '50s auto dealers had heavy showroom traffic even without using promotion. The newly designed models that fit new suburban lifestyles were the draw. Reprinted with permission.

EXHIBIT 1.2 Maidenform established its "brand image" by addressing women's most intimate fantasies. Reprinted with permission.

EXHIBIT 1.3 As television moved into almost every American home, it became a status symbol with manufacturers promoting their sleek designs and "high style." Reprinted with permission.

- Average steel workers earned $75/week in 1952.
- "I Love Lucy" was the number one television show, 1952–57.
- Polaroid produced 12 million pairs of 3-D glasses a month in 1953.
- The Corvette was introduced in 1954.
- By 1954, 34 manufacturers were licensed to produce Campbell Kids items, including children's cookware, books, paper dolls, bicycles, and clothes.
- A study in the magazine *Supermarket Merchandising* showed 3,000 new supermarkets with an average size of 16,000 square feet were planned for 1956.
- An estimated 5,000 new grocery items were planned for those new supermarkets.
- 400 million frozen pot pies were eaten in 1958.
- President Eisenhower's favorite dessert was Prune Whip.

The Decade of Cardboard Salesmen

There were no sales promotion agencies in the '50s. There were display companies, like Einson-Freeman and Rapid Mounting. There were display brokers who would sell the works of display companies and artists. There were huge, top-notch art studios where teams of artists would render photo-quality artwork and client-specific comps. But there were no sales promotion agencies.

Clients did much of their own promotion planning and execution, from prevalent on-pack or mail-in premiums (who can forget all the wonderful toys available on cereal boxes?) to popular contests for jingles and slogans. Advertising agencies also did much of their own promotion, as a lot of the new television advertising was, in fact, promotion.

I started with one of Chicago's biggest art studios, Kling Studios, basically as an art and display salesman, then as a copywriter. Both jobs gave me a good perspective on the business. It was much simpler then and lots of fun. Let me share with you how life in promotions was back in the early days of supermarkets and suburbia.

Land of Plenty

After the shortages and hardships of the wars, people wanted to buy things. Everything. All the new gadgets like televisions and hand mixers. And with so many new products in the stores, retailers depended heavily on manufacturers' marketing materials to help their salesmen sell and customers buy. So we sold cardboard displays and ''sales aids''—flipcharts, sell sheets, catalogs, pocket pieces, etc.—to manufacturers. We became cardboard salesmen.

Studios tended to specialize in certain industries. Kling did major appliances, others did automotive, packaged goods, or straight retail. Sears controlled the largest studio in town with all the materials they required. But in the booming Midwest, we had as much business as we wanted with Chicago companies. I later launched my own business with appliance and television manufacturers as the base.

''Investment Spending''

Speculation was the rule of the day. There were no retainers, no consulting fees. Clients wanted to buy ''stuff'' and for you to sell anything, you needed to invest a little upfront. If you sold a display for which you had comped a spec, you would probably get the job to do collateral materials with it. So each display sold was a big piece of business. And displays weren't cheap, as you'd have to recoup the creative expenses for all the displays you *didn't* sell. One agency claimed they had to sell every third display they did on spec to make enough money to stay in business.

Everyone did ''spec'' work. Roy Reents of Rapid Display and Mounting, one of Chicago's largest and most respected display construction companies, claims his company would overrun 50 blank displays when running a job for a company. These "blanks" would be passed around to the display brokers in town who would then take them to art studios to be turned into display ideas. Each of the different brokers would deliver a different creative idea on the comp, so they were all selling a fresh display from the same basic structure.

The spec situation brought about some classic "under the table" abuses. Though the majority of clients were above board, the opportunities for kickbacks were ever present. Consider the situation. An agency brings in a speculative display idea that as yet does not have a firm price. The client likes it, asks about price, which at that point, could be manipulated to include something under the table. We learned to stay away from the big boys expecting kickback options, as there were plenty of long-term, honest clients around.

Sales Calls

There were no agencies of record then, so we would often run into our competitors at key accounts. And we found that the first one into a client's office often got the sale. So we started getting up and on the road earlier and earlier in hopes of offering clients the best ideas first. On top of that, Rapid and the other display companies were selling to clients directly.

I remember calling on Schlitz Beer with a great idea only to be told that Roy Reents from Rapid had been there with the same construction the previous week. But that didn't happen often and we were such a close knit family, you overlooked these "coincidences."

Another way clients would make decisions on which display to buy was to bring in a secretary and ask her. In the male bastian of business in those days, it was thought that a female secretary would be a little closer to the tastes of the homemaker the display was often designed to attract. Pure whim awarded some very large and important display contracts.

Most often however, you won the business based on creativity and personal chemistry. If they liked you, you got in the door. Then if they liked the idea, they bought it.

Our clients were very different in the '50s. Brand management had not come into power yet. We called on advertising managers and promotion managers, who were usually very amazing guys. They not only had responsibility for ad and displays but planned the sales meetings and wrote and delivered speeches. They wrote their own copy between reviewing media plans and setting our publicity programs. The good guys were really great! A personal favorite was Erik Isgrig, Vice President of Advertising at Zenith who was the stereotypical client, rewriting new and improved copy until the project went to press—yet always fair and thoughtful. And he wore electric blue suits!

How Did We Charge?

One reason we had such ongoing good relationships with clients is we seldom got into sticky pricing situations. When we told a client how much a display would cost, we stuck to that figure. Of course, we would always charge for alterations and overruns, but never could we come back and say that the motor or lights or artwork cost more than we had planned.

We lived with our estimates because we brought all the critical parties together for estimating. A typical estimating scenario would include an art director, a printer, a keyline/type/production specialist, a display construction estimator, and the account or sales guy. We would usually start with a set figure, perhaps $10.00 per unit, and figure out what we could build for that. Then the art director began with an idea. The printer suggested paper stock and size. The construction estimator added lights and motion motors. The production specialist anticipated type and illustration costs. The account guy suggested spangles and trim. Then they added it all up, saw how close they came to the $10.00 limit and cut where needed. Maybe a slight size modification could put more displays on a sheet press, allowing less paper waste. Or perhaps a less expensive motor might be used. Or a change in art style could help hold costs. The key was that everyone involved was included and could make cost-cutting suggestions upfront. And they committed to that cost. Obviously, this estimating method came before corporate mandates for three alternative bids and unknown suppliers. It was unthinkable to give the job to someone other than the folks that helped you estimate the price or work on the spec comp. We all were investing our time and talents equally into the job because we all knew we would benefit from the win.

The Promotion Atmosphere in the Fifties

The '50s were, for marketing, an unsophisticated time. The marketplace was open, with consumers clamoring to buy all they could. There was much less pressure on the bottom line than there is today, with a general feeling that there was money enough for everyone to prosper. Doing business was very direct, without committees and lines of authority. The people we called on were smart and were the decision-makers. And consequently the business moved faster—and gave us all time to go out and invent the three-martini lunch. The entertainment part of the business was just as important as the pricing part. Customers often bought on personality as much as price.

There were more ''characters'' in the business then—high energy, bright men willing to take some risks and do investment spending. And there were a stable of characters and good friends who continue in the business in Chicago. There's Dick Adams with Feldkamp-Malloy art studios who saw the industry grow from all handlettering and lavish photo-illustration to computer wizardry. And John Lindar who never speculated more than $10.00 on a job in his career (printers didn't have to. . .). And Hugh Lambert who learned the display and promotion business in the '40s and still brings his expertise to Promotional Marketing, Inc. as Senior Vice President. And Roy Reents from Rapid who will soon be retiring after a career in building displays for every industry in America.

We were good business associates and close friends. And anyone in this business knows how important your valuable associates are to your success—much more important than the lowest bidder.

"God Forbid"

This is a story that tells what entrepreneurship is all about. It's about risk. In 1958, Roy Knipschild and I decided it was time to part company. So we tossed a coin to see who would buy the other one out and I won the honor of going into debt. Like a shopkeeper who quietly pays for merchandise from the $20 bills under the cash register tray, I lifted up my tray of all my, and the company's available funds, most of which was earmarked for current payables, and paid Roy all my money (and then some) for the business. I was then looking at a totally empty cash register.

Looking back, I am amazed at the gumption it took to ask my employees and suppliers to stick with me through this cash flow crisis. And that brings us to "God Forbid."

There were four very important suppliers I approached to help me float until I could stand on my own. I looked at my receivables (as they did) and set up a plan that would pay back all I owed plus interest within 30 months. Then I took it to my creditors for their blessing.

Once a month I would have dinner with each of my guardian angels, Bob Hoover and Dick Kern from Hoover & Kern Art Studios, John Lindar from Alco Printing and Paper Box Co., Don Deering from Rayner Litho and Jules Abramson, owner and Walter Neuman, president of Rapid Mounting and Display Co. We would review my cash position and I would give them a check for what I could afford that month.

It was Jules Abramson, however, who took my plight the most seriously. I owed him about $35,000—$40,000, a very small amount of money in terms of the size of his business. Yet each month as we reviewed the book he said the same things: "That's very good that you can give us that much money, Bill, because if something should happen to you, God forbid, then we, God forbid, would never, God forbid, get our money back, God forbid."

To this day, I double check our books to make sure we are on top of payments to Rapid whenever I hear anyone say "God forbid." And the happy outcome of the story is I beat my payback plan by six months.

In the meantime I learned some very important lessons I'm happy to share with any aspiring entrepreneurs:

1. Your suppliers *want* to keep you in business.
2. It never hurts to *ask*.
3. Take very good care of yourself when you owe money so that, *God forbid*, nothing happens to you.

Salesmanship According to Ben Bills

The most important part of our business doesn't happen at retail, media, or during a broker presentation. It comes much earlier when we approach a prospective client. We start by selling and then keep selling. We sell while delivering our creative recommendations. And sell display specs and materials. We sell our company with every follow-up call responding to lost shipments or reprint queries.

But it's the first face-to-face encounter with a client that stands out most in my mind. And mastering the art of selling in these situations sets you up to sell forever. I'm including this section as a "Lucky Strike Extra"—as a helpful guide for anyone in the business who wants to sell. The timeless advice here helps you think about the process. And I guarantee it works as well now as it did in the '50s!

I met Benjamin Franklin Bills in the late '50s when I came back from the service. He taught a course called "Salesmanship" at Northwestern University night school, having made his fortune in the real estate market in Chicago. I took the course on the G.I. Bill and ended up teaching with him for four or five years.

What Ben Bills taught was to discover how people buy. Once you understand how people buy, then you can understand how to sell to them. I still use Ben's approaches to selling today and pass these on to our agency people. See how Ben's timeless methods can work for you.

Three Major Functions in Preparing for and Making the Sale

Sales don't begin in the buyer's office but begin in the seller's mind. These steps are critical every time you approach *any* account and not just on your initial call.

1. *Analyzing.* Plan what you can reasonably accomplish with the buyer at each succeeding sales call. These accomplishments may be getting your buyer to believe in your company's services or abilities; getting a trial order; getting a request for a proposal; selling the next presentation; etc. In this step, you dig out the features and benefits about your product that you believe may cause the buyer to act.
2. *Organizing.* Plan the presentation order of your features and benefits so that you can get enough benefits in front of your buyer to say *yes*, without giving him a chance to say *no*.
3. *Presenting.* Deliver what you set out in Steps 1 and 2 to the buyer. Specifically, this step should stress the distinctive facts and benefits that will make your product or service

standout, in your buyer's mind, as superior or different from the competition.

How People Buy: The Eight Buying Moods in Which Buyers React

Once you establish how someone will buy, then you know how to sell. Depending on their mood, buyers are influenced by different degrees of sensation, reason, and emotion. Intellectual moods call for more reasoning power; fast-paced, impatient moods call for ''show-me'' sensationalism, and so forth.

Buyers generally fall into the following eight moods, each mood calling for a different degree of sensation, reason, or emotion. Take note, however, that buyers' moods change, sometimes within a single sales call. Different circumstances, different products, different developments in the interview influence your buyer's moods.

1. *The Even-Minded Normal.* Generally open-minded, willing to listen. Cautious but considerate. Use equal appeals to sensations that suggest to him or her the idea to buy; reasons which develop this idea to buy; emotions which impel the buyer into action.

2. *The Impulse-Minded Emotional.* Prejudice-minded; strongly for or against matters. Sensations and reasons are less influential than with #1; use emotions.

3. *A Rigid-Minded Professional.* Set-minded, positive on specifications and needs. This buyer ''goes by the book.'' Use reasons and facts, the more rigid and to his or her specs, the better.

4. *Creative-Minded Intellectual.* Imaginative as to his or her needs; exploratory-minded and somewhat distrustful of set specs; contemplates a better way. Use creative reasons or sensations.

5. *Smart-Minded Intellectual.* Quips, puns, and wisecracks; is agile-minded. This buyer will be impressed with sensa-

tions as openers but sold later with reasons or emotions.

6. *Grunter Negative.* Apt to not say much of anything; is unresponsive and aloof. Keep probing to find his or her ''buyer hot buttons.''

7. *Gusher Negative.* Strong on promise but weak on performance; tends to mislead you into thinking you have a ''sure sale,'' yet seldom buys. Usually has some hidden reason for inaction. See if you can find others to corroborate or see if you can find the real decision maker.

8. *Skeptical-Minded Negative.* Starts arguing ''why not'' before you can begin with ''why''; immediately takes the offensive. Do not argue back, but stay with it to see if he or she is testing you. This person may later turn into a buyer.

Assessing the buyer's mood early on in the presentation allows you to target the appeal that fits the moment for a much more compelling delivery.

The Five Talking Steps

You've planned your presentation, you've organized your features and benefits, you've assessed your buyer's mood. Now comes the delivery, the most critical part. Remember each of the delivery steps by memorizing the first letter of each ''C-SEC-C.''

1. *Comparison.* Find a favorable situation that your prospect can identify with. ''May I tell you about a program we just completed for the XYZ company that may be similar to what you're facing?''

2. *Suggestions.* Qualify the prospect to make sure that this is the type of benefit he or she is interested in. ''Ms. Jones, would this type of program be helpful to your brand?''

3. *Explanation.* List and describe the features and benefits of your product. ''You could save considerable precious staff time by consolidating your promotion program.''

4. *Confirmation*. Draw upon other successful situations to make the prospects feel comfortable. "ABC company used a similar solution that saved them $x in overtime."
5. *Close*. The winning step. If you've done the above steps, from comparison through confirmation, you're in a good position to close: "Will Tuesday or Thursday be the best day to see you with our proposal?"

I've read, tried, memorized, and taught many other sales techniques, but I've never found a purer, easier, more predictable process than Ben Bills!

Signs of the Times—A Fifties Sampler of Promotions

In searching for representative examples from the '50s, I was truly surprised to see so many promotions similar to those we see today. These samples were chosen to be representative of the times.

Johnson's Wax—Glo-Coat Bonus Can

In the days when a woman was judged by the shine on her new kitchen floor in suburbia, bonus pack offers of extra product carried considerable weight. Here, Johnson Wax promised enough extra product to polish two average floors free in its "Big Get-Acquainted Bonus Can." (See Exhibit 1.4.)

Whirlpool Washers/All Detergent— Free Sample

The new-home boom of suburbia in the '50s meant booming sales of major appliances. Washers and dryers led the way with

EXHIBIT 1.4

models designed for all price ranges and places—even "conspicuous first-floor locations" for the new ranch homes.

Detergents recognized the sampling opportunity with new laundry equipment sales and offered free samples packed into all appliance purchases. Here All detergent enjoyed an implied endorsement from the manufacturer and its Home Laundry Institute. (See Exhibit 1.5.)

Parkay Margarine—TV Jingle Contest

Early tie-in efforts with RCA Color Televisions brought real excitement to Kraft's Parkay Margarine. In 1955, 45 color TV prizes were certain to catch the eye of jingle writers. While Parkay's product features seem quite antiquated today— "Won't tear fresh bread, even when cold"—the contest prize value still works.

RCA and Kraft both got additional exposure with this promotion. Contestants visited their RCA dealer or grocer for more details, so we could expect contest displays at each location. (See Exhibit 1.6.)

Borden Company—Elsie the Cow

In the early 1950s a consumer survey was done to identify the strength of trademark figures. Elsie the Cow, Borden Co.'s dairy symbol ranked third following Aunt Jemima and the Bird's Eye kids. What could be more natural than to offer Elsie as a self-liquidating premium for $2.50 plus a Borden's Ice Cream carton flap?

Plush renditions of trademarks continued to grow in promotion offers. As a way to get young customers familiar with your brand and keep them loyal, there's no better way than to offer your symbol as a lovable doll. (Did you know Elsie had a husband, Elmer, who was the inspiration for Borden's Glue Company?) (See Exhibit 1.7.)

EXHIBIT 1.5

EXHIBIT 1.6

EXHIBIT 1.7

Courtesy of Vicki Linder, Sales Solutions

Baby Ruth/Curtiss Candies—Free Flower Seeds

This is a great example of how borrowed interest was a standard promotion tactic even back in 1955. A spring promotion perennial, free seeds have promoted many products over time because of their universal appeal, low cost and perceived value. (See Exhibit 1.8.)

The Creative Side of the Fifties

My great theory for a winning Christmas display was to take three elements—a grandfather with a white beard, a dog wagging his tail and a little baby with its pajama trap door unbuttoned—and rearrange them every year. You couldn't lose with these three elements.

And in keeping with the decade when consumers bought eveything they could, clients bought creative thinking like this. Christmas displays with grandfathers, wagging-tailed dogs, and bare-bottomed babies gaily decorated stores across America.

It seems as if there was no accounting for people's taste in this decade. As we have seen, clients often selected display designs on the whims of their secretaries or wives. Or a new material, a new way to use motion (the waving clown becomes the ear-wagging cow), or spangles and shims could win an order from a client who simply wanted something different.

Hugh Lambert, a brilliant and creative art director for 20 years, recounts how he learned "layout surgery."

"There was a sequence for selling a display. First, we would comp it up for Zenith, complete with the tagline, 'The quality goes in before the name goes on.' And there was no Presstype or color stats at the time so everything was hand rendered.

EXHIBIT 1.8

"If Bill couldn't sell it to Zenith, he'd bring back the comp and we would painfully remove that logo and render in Motorola's logo. If Motorola didn't buy it, we'd give Admiral a shot. Our last resort was down-and-dirty Philco, the cheapest. By then, the comp was beginning to show signs of wear in the logo area. So, if Philco didn't buy it, we'd toss the construction. Clearly this preceded the days of brand image."

Once you come up with a novel, creative idea, why waste it? Those were the days when we tried to get a lot of mileage out of all our ideas.

Bringing TV to Retail

What we saw on television we tried to translate into our displays. We would build displays around either the advertising or the advertised product features. Frigidaire washers had agitators that went up and down, so we built elaborate motion displays that showed this *exclusive* feature. Point of sale materials would call out every single feature and gizmo of these *new* and *improved* products, a tag put on most items whether they were improved or even changed. Bombastic products claims were standard as manufacturers persuaded you in the store to buy their brand.

Displays also performed a truly informative function, explaining how really new and improved products worked. Homemakers had heard about garbage disposals but marveled at display simulations showing how they actually worked. And real improvements were happening in our household cleaners and packaged foods that needed to be told. Yet it was often hard for a consumer to distinguish the truth from the hype at point of sale, just as in television advertising.

And just like on television, retail stores everywhere were filled with life-size cutouts of advertising spokespeople. A General Electric cutout of Ronald Reagan inviting customers to check out the appliances he talked about on the weekly "GE Theater" stands out as a creative director's (and Hugh Lambert's) nightmare.

"Reagan was photographed in a tan suit, which looked very handsome but it was very difficult to control the color on press—especially in life-size. In those days, with the unsophisticated press equipment, a pressman could sneeze and shift an entire run of color. So if they got Reagan's suit right, his skintones would look bad. If his flesh was the right color, his suit would look blotchy.

"On top of this, Reagan was photographed from above—which would be fine in a small print ad or display. But as a lifesize cutout, it appeared as if he was going to fall forward on to the store's customers. And as another sign of the times, the client found these off-color, off-balance displays to be totally *acceptable*. How our standards and technology have improved since then!"

Contests: "In 25 Words or Less. . . "

What would your last line to this jingle be?

"Dogs are funny, that's easy to see
Whether 'mixed-up mutt' or pedigree,
But when Chow Time comes, they're sure to be
_____."

There was a $20,000 first prize ready to be awarded by Purina for the best answer here. Jingles and slogan contests were the rage in the '50s, always aimed at persuading consumers to use the product before filling in the answer "in 25 words or less."

In today's fast-paced world, the sweepstakes and contest hobbyists seem to be the only ones who find time to enter thought-provoking contests such as these. But in the leisurely '50s, contest-entering was a creative, involving pastime.

We've moved on to plenty of exciting and creative contests and sweepstakes since the jingle-writing craze. For instance in 1975 Schick asked men to "Send Your Face To Schick"—certainly an unusual and clever request. In return for submitting a photo, men were entered into a sweepstakes that awarded a grand prize of $25,000 plus $1,000 a year for life. And the first 50,000 entrants received a free Schick razor and trial pack of blades (a great way to sample future blade purchases). All this was done to call attention to Schick's new "Love Your Face" ad campaign.

One of the longest running and most respected contests got its start in 1949 as "The Grand National Recipe and Baking Contest." The Pillsbury Bake-Off Contest focused on the ingenuity of homemakers and their ability to turn Pillsbury's packaged cake mixes into special desserts. As Pillsbury's product line grew, so did the recipe categories. In the 1990 21st Pillsbury Bake-Off, contestants could enter any of these categories—appetizers, desserts, microwave entrees, light meal and kid's cooking, supporting Pillsbury's refrigerated and frozen products as well as the classic packaged cake mixes. Pillsbury has effectively translated the event into a vehicle for storewide displays and consumer FSI promotions as well as having a constant influx of new recipes.

Over the years some of the most creative efforts have gone into the prizes. You could "Win the car of Ringo Starr" from Craig car stereos in 1978. Or perhaps win a 1976 Kiss rock concert for your school from M&M/Mars. Benson & Hedges has always let us choose from 100 prizes, whether 100 pounds of jelly beans or 100 inches of Ford Mustang. Kool cigarettes gave away a Rolls-Royce Corniche. Max cigarettes let you choose a fur by your favorite designer.

More recently cable station VH-1 awarded a Corvette Collection of 36 classic cars. And British Airways gave away the best of London with shopping sprees to Harrod's, a London townhouse, a Rolls-Royce, and over 500 free trips to London.

But creatively it's hard to top Parker Bros. prize for celebrating the 40th birthday of Monopoly in 1973. They simply replaced the Monopoly money with $15,000 in cash.

Involvement with the product has been important in getting consumers to buy the product, not just enter the sweepstakes. So we've seen "match and win" games where you match an FSI to a display. Or match a game piece to the actual product or package. Glad Wrap sent you to the supermarket in 1965, magazine ads in hand, to match a "4" on a price-off package snipe.

Game pieces have been put inside packages, the most memorable being in Cracker Jack in 1981. The popcorn treat known for the surprise inside took that concept further by packing chances to win station wagons filled with toys!

Valvoline sent you to your favorite auto store every week in 1978 to try your luck in an NFL weekly football pool. Retailers loved the traffic. And Valvoline loved the display and sales they got from 16 straight weeks of fresh weekly sweepstakes.

Fame has often been a motivator in "search" contests. Susan Anton was crowned "Miss Muriel Cigars" in 1976, taking over the role of sexy spokeswoman from Edie Adams. The Breck Girl, the St. Pauli Girl, Miss Black Velvet, and Playboy's Anniversary Hunt Playmates have all been found through various photo contests.

There are hundreds of examples of contests and sweepstakes "classics." And they all point to the effectiveness of using a dream to capture attention for your product or service.

But of all the games in the past, perhaps the strangest contest ever run has to be the 1988 Benson & Hedges pajama contest. It was magazine readers who brought on the contest, having seen an unusual B & H ad and writing to Philip Morris asking what was going on in the ad's photo. The photo shows a table of formally dressed diners with a hip-looking man clad only in pajama bottoms having wandered onto the scene. Readers were asked to enter by sending their guess of what was happening in the photo. The prizes? Pajamas, of course.

EXHIBIT 1.9 The 1990 Pillsbury Bake-Off was the most recent in the long series for this biennial recipe contest. Reprinted with permission.

EXHIBIT 1.10 VH-1 cable TV station captured the imaginations of its target audience by giving away 36 Corvettes to one winner. Reprinted with permission.

EXHIBIT 1.11 Glad Wrap's sweepstakes sent shoppers to compare their LOOK magazine game piece to the price-off violator on the package in stores. Reprinted with permission.

NEW TEXTURED GLAD WRAP ANNOUNCES...

$400,000 Match-the-"4" Sweepstakes

4¢ OFF
Price marked is **4¢ OFF** *regular price*

100 FOOT ROLL
Plastic Food Wrap

THIS "4" MIGHT BE WORTH $400 FOR YOU!
Take it to the store (or see Rule #2 below). Match it with the "4" on an actual package of new Textured GLAD Wrap—and see.

1,000 PRIZES ☀ $400 EACH
you may be looking at a winner right on this page!

Here's how the Match-the-"4" Sweepstakes works. Up above you'll find a picture of the package of new Textured GLAD Wrap. On the package in the picture it says "4¢ OFF."

If the "4" on the package shown in this ad matches EXACTLY (in style, shape and size) the "4" on the "4¢ OFF"

sign on an actual package you'll find at any supermarket (or the facsimile available as per Rule #2)—*you've won $400!* There are 1,000 prizes—and you might be looking at a winner right now! So check up—and find out. It would be a shame to miss out on 400 free dollars, wouldn't it?

HERE'S HOW YOU WIN—OFFICIAL RULES

1. $400,000 is waiting to be claimed! A thousand winning ads are in magazines just like this one all across the country. You may have a winner right here!
2. Take this ad to your store (or see below). "Match-the-4" by holding the 4 on the package in your ad up to the 4¢ OFF sign on a Textured GLAD Wrap package. You can take just the picture of the package to the store, if you wish. If the 4 in your ad matches exactly (in style, shape and size) the 4 on the Textured GLAD Wrap package, you're a $400 winner. You only have to check one package to find out. Or, send a stamped, self-addressed envelope to "GLAD" Sweepstakes, Box 127, New York, N. Y. 10046, for an exact facsimile of the "4" as it appears on the new Textured GLAD Wrap package.
3. If you have a winning "4," send it — together with your name and address—by

registered mail to the judging organization, D. L. Blair Corp., 38 E. 29th St., New York, N. Y. 10016. Upon verification of your winning ad, you will receive $400.
4. Sweepstakes closes December 15, 1965. All winning claims must be postmarked by that date and must be received by January 5, 1966.
5. Only one winner per family.
6. Decision of the judges is final.
7. Sweepstakes not open to employees (or their families) of Union Carbide Corporation, its advertising agencies, magazines publishing this advertisement and their production agents, or the judging organization.
8. Prize offer good in U.S.A., but void in Nebraska and wherever else prohibited by law.

New Textured* GLAD Wrap has *cling control*. You can crumple new Textured GLAD Wrap into a ball and the tiny tangle-control channels make it easier to handle. When you want it to cling—it does. And it clings without tangling. Self-sealing. And 100 feet of new Textured GLAD Wrap costs no more than 50 feet of the high-priced kind. *Cling control*, 100 feet instead of 50. That's *Freshness Plus*. So try a package of new Textured GLAD Wrap today. You'll like it! You get an extra savings of 4¢ off. And you may win $400!

GLAD is a registered trade mark of

UNION CARBIDE
Pioneers in Plastics

*PATENT PENDING

EXHIBIT 1.12 Benson & Hedges cigarettes received so many queries about the man in pajamas in this ad that the company created a contest for smokers to speculate on the situation. Reprinted with permission.

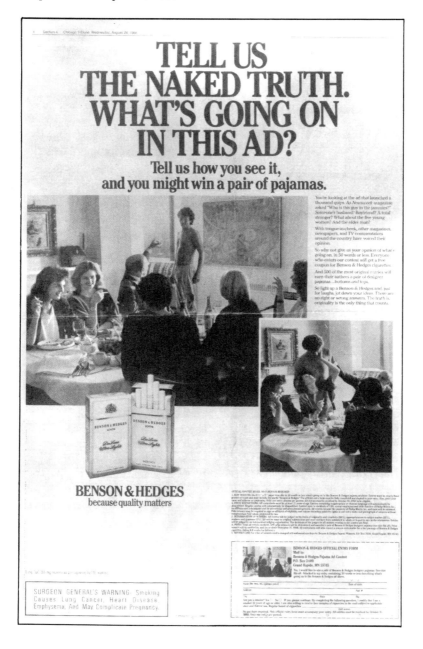

Lessons from the Fifties

The fifties live on. What have we brought with us from this Golden Age of Display?

- Motion displays—we're using the same motion machines and simple technology light sources. However slight, we've seen improvements in the long-lasting energy sources.
- Lifesize cutouts—based on a desire for a stronger in-store presence, cutouts continue to enjoy sporadic flashes of popularity. The Bartles & James Wine Cooler front porch display brought back cutouts in the 1980s. And cost realities made the lifesize trend fade. But we know it will surface again, like all the display basics.
- Keep trying—just like selling displays in the past, if you knock on enough doors today with a good display comp, you'll eventually find someone to buy it.
- Products that fill a need sell—when consumers needed to furnish houses, when suburban chores required transportation, we bought those products that fit our needs. No matter how great a promotion, if a product "doesn't work," it won't sell.

CHAPTER TWO

The Sixties— Change, Change, Change

This was the decade America lost her innocence. It was ten years of vibrant dichotomies—of a proud nation watching John Glenn in space while headlines told of Freedom Trains and race riots in the South. News reports interrupted the frivolous, top-rated TV show, "Laugh-In," to bring word of the mayhem in Chicago during the Democratic Convention and a battle between the police and the Yippies. While assassins were bringing an end to "Camelot," the Beatles stormed America, a man walked on the moon, and civil rights legislation was passed.

Images of Change

The decade of change was brought about with the help of these significant trends:

1. The power surge of television.
2. The impact of the baby boom beginnings.
3. The end of the homemaker.

The Power of Television

The influence of television on the American family started the decade strong and grew as we saw how TV could bring us the news as it happened. The weekend of sorrow surrounding President John F. Kennedy's death let us see what a powerful medium we had.

Suddenly, newsmakers, politicians, and marketers could entertain, influence and persuade people faster than ever before with action and sound. The media could be manipulated to convince the masses of almost anything. Where in the past, uprisings may have received passing attention in delayed news reels and newspapers, now action could be reported as it happened.

This was the era of "The Happening"—staged media events that ranged from the Freedom Riders in 1961 who traveled from Washington DC to New Orleans testing the treatment of negroes along the way, to Woodstock, the 4-day music, drug, free love fest that symbolized the dreams of the huge population of young people. We turned to our television sets to see Neil Armstrong walk on the moon in 1969, just two days after our morning news had reported the death of Mary Jo Kopechne, a passenger in the car of Senator Edward Kennedy when he drove off the bridge of Chappaquiddick Island.

Television no longer only showed us life with Lucy and the Cleavers but brought us footage from Vietnam. This raised doubts of the sanctity of our public officials and nation, and made great viewing. And the Neilsen scores of TV viewership soared.

No significant product was advertised without having television be a major part of the budget. The impact of national television on new product introductions or image campaigns was critical for success. Clutter was already an issue in advertising, as adman Leo Bogart wrote in 1967, "Every day 4.2 billion advertising messages pour forth . . ." Products were easy to launch with a ready market looking for the new, convenient packaged goods and advanced technology appliances seen on television.

Enter, the Flower Children

We also began to see the changes brought on by the baby boom— the bump in population of the children born after the wars. This surge of young people meant more schools in the '60s, more economic power of teenagers and youth (especially to buy the records and the trappings of the Beatles and other British-invasion pop artists), and a louder voice for the young.

This was the first generation to grow up with television as its source of news, culture, and entertainment. Rather than accept the world as Ricky Nelson saw it, this group witnessed first hand the assassinations of its leaders, the corruption of public officials, and civil strife in the South.

The idealism of youth was the perfect venue for social change. Sit-ins became standard procedures for college students bent on being heard. The sit-in had begun with the civil rights workers in the South and later served as a standard tactic for protest against everything from chemical warfare in Vietnam to demanding co-ed visitation in women's dorms. And with powerful television coverage behind this tactic, students could win their battles.

Flower power was an emerging economic power as young people found their own art styles in pop art, their own music in the San Francisco and British sounds, and a new interest in ''natural'' things. While this baby boom group would grow even larger and more economically influential in later decades, the youth of the '50s was the most powerful in waking up the nation.

Liberation for Women

While protesters were demanding equal rights for everyone and women were soon to burn bras for liberation, it was technological advances that brought an end to vacuuming while wearing pearls. Credit the availability of birth control pills and the invention of panty hose for the real opportunities of liberation.

Though birth control did not become widely accepted until late in the decade, the fact that women could take control of their child-bearing futures made a major impact on their entrance into the work world. Suddenly, women were able to select the role of mother and worker (careers were still not for women). The first step opened the doors for women to demand better job opportunities and pay as the excuse of ''motherhood'' could no longer stand in employers' ways.

More personally liberating was the introduction of panty hose and the release from girdles and garters. This opened up fashion options including pantsuits and the mini-skirt, which kept getting shorter as the decade progressed. Plus women could buy these new panty hose at increasingly convenient supermarket or the new discount stores that were opening in every suburb. As silly as it seems, panty hose truly freed women from the constriction of fashion and symbolically let them concentrate on more important issues.

The Decade of Change

The '60s came in like a lamb with the economy and patriotism on a high. And they left like a furious lion with students in revolt, an unfulfilling war and distrust of our public officials. Things happened faster in the '60s than any previous decade because we saw

EXHIBIT 2.1 The '60s started out as a pleasant extension of the conservative '50s as seen in this ad for a 1961 Brownie Starmeter camera from Kodak. Reprinted courtesy Eastman Kodak Company.

EXHIBIT 2.2 Marketing turned psychedelic following the popularity of the Beatles, Pop Art and Peter Max. Even Crackers went wild in 1966. Reprinted with permission.

them happen in our own homes. We moved into the '70s with a new awareness of our ecology, politics, and outer space. And with new products like panty hose, stereo sound, imported cars, dishwashers and Xerox copiers. We made the transition with a sophisticated distrust that replaced our naivety of the '50s.

Facts from the Sixties

■ Xerox copiers were introduced in 1960.

■ The 1960 U.S. budget was set at $79.4 billion with a $4.2 billion surplus.

■ General Motors' 1965 revenues of $20 billion came just under those of Britain and France.

■ In 1966 Truman Capote gave a party for 540 "close friends" in New York.

■ The acclaimed sales promotion agency, Glendenning Co. of Westport, CT, set up Danbury Mint to offer limited edition commemorative medals recognizing Neil Armstrong's walk on the moon in 1969.

■ By 1962, there were 2,000 discount stores in the U.S.

■ Kimberly-Clark offered a throwaway paper dress for $1.00 and a box-top. The matching "go-go boots" and "mad mod cap" were extra.

■ S & W Green Stamps sales hit an all-time high of $369 million in 1969.

The Procter Way to Success

Whether employees or competitors of Procter & Gamble, most marketers believe that P&G's strategically focused and consistently applied marketing is the key factor to the company's success. Add to this superior product quality, a remarkable sales force, unrelenting sales promotion, and the "deep pockets" required to investment-spend against opportunities with three-year-payouts, and it's easy to see how they were able to launch and support so many leadership brands. A classic story of P&G doing all the right things is the introduction and expansion of Bounty Towels. This story also shows how promotion played a vital role in the overall plan.

Charmin Led the Way

Procter & Gamble got into the paper products business in the late 1950s by acquiring a small regional manufacturer, the Charmin Company, based in Green Bay, Wisconsin. Using Charmin's midwestern distribution area as a large test market, P&G went to work learning everything they could about the paper market products, the sales potential, and consumer wants.

The paper towel category held much promise, but P&G was patient until the company was able to develop a product with a meaningful consumer point of difference. Meanwhile, its largest competitor, ScotTowels, held an approximate 50 percent share.

In 1965, Bounty Towels were introduced into two small test markets—Columbus, Ohio and Wichita, Kansas—where the brand achieved market leadership within six months. These results convinced P&G to use Bounty as its lead brand in expanding its paper products nationwide.

Promotion played a major role in the marketing of Bounty. The first objective was trial, to build credibility behind the superior absorbancy claims and to get early consumer acceptance. So P&G began expensive but successful full-roll sampling. No company had ever used this high-cost sampling approach. However, it proved so successful for P&G that they expanded full-roll delivery, adding coupons to further encourage initial purchase.

While the consumer activities were in full swing, Procter worked on the trade. Off-invoice allowances were given to encourage distribution. Case allowances were added for merchandising and display support. And to ensure in-store trial, off-price packs were used for introductions.

With full-roll sampling, bounceback coupons, trade distribution, and merchandising allowances and price packs, the promotion component for Bounty's introduction was complete. Value-added promotions were to be incorporated quickly into Bounty's promotional mix, including a tie-in with household cleaners and a self-liquidator for a cleaning caddy.

Add powerful advertising and positioning for the quicker-picker-upper and P&G had a true product success. Even more important was the category growth spurred on by the Bounty introduction. Year One paper towel market growth ranged from 19 to 42 percent, proof to America's retailers that Procter & Gamble meant business!

Paper towel market leaders, 1990

Brand	Supermarket sales (in millions)
1. Bounty	$383.3
2. ScotTowels	208.1
3. Brawny	142.6

Bounty was just one of the gangbuster products introduced by P&G in the '60s. We also got Pampers, Charmin, Safeguard, Folgers, Secret, and more. And each new brand got sampling, market development funds, advertising and retailer support that guaranteed success.

The Vendor Side of P&G

As an "idea salesman," doing business with Procter & Gamble in the '60s was great! It was a time of unbridled growth both creatively and volume-wise. Here you had *so* much business—so many brands all challenged with maximizing potential. Couple that with a marketplace that truly was excited about the newest advances in toothpaste and detergent. The possibilities were endless.

During the '60s we saw the growth of the entire paper business with P&G. Charmin and Bounty were one area where we saw significant product improvements. Even bigger was the launch of a whole new category—disposable diapers—with the introduction of Pampers in 1966. Clearly there was plenty of challenge for a hardworking creative shop with a big art bag.

We would start at 8 a.m. on Monday in Cincinnati with a case filled with work that had been ordered the previous Monday. We'd make the rounds dropping off display layouts or sell sheet keylines, calling on the creative director in each division. And picking up new assignments and purchase orders as we went. At 4:20 as we left headquarters to catch the last flight out, we'd have another full art bag to keep the crew in Chicago busy. It was a heyday for people willing to get up early and work hard. If you had two or three great ideas to take with you on Monday mornings, you were guaranteed work for the week. And because everyone was on commission, the week always ended ''in the black.''

Now, P&G was not buying great strategic thinking or promotional recommendations. That's what they paid their corps of MBAs for. They were buying ''stuff.'' Pictures and creative display ideas. Attention getting headlines and visuals. And hundreds of ways to say ''new,'' ''save,'' and ''try.''

While P&G was learning from coupon results and product movement, the ''vendors'' were learning new production techniques and improved communication devices. It was strictly a vendor/buyer relationship at the time, typical of the strictly proprietary operation that has launched so many consumer marketing winners.

Signs of the Times—A Sixties Sampler of Promotions

Volkswagen—Bonds for Babies Born in Volkswagens

Corvette and Porsche owners may have their own club to compare radials and talk torque. And Edsel and Corvair collectors gather to evaluate their investments. But perhaps the most exclusive club in the world was founded as a promotional gimmick for Volkswagen. In 1964, Volkswagen announced it would present all babies born in VWs with a gift of U.S. Savings Bonds and permanent membership in the "Bonds for Babies Born in Volkswagens Club." While club benefits are scarce and there isn't a key to the clubhouse, prestigious membership has been bestowed on over 500 babies since the program's beginning.

As a testament to the popularity of the VW van in the days of flower children, the club racked up its most members in one year—44 babies born in Volkswagens in 1969. VWs became the favorite auto of midwives as they could enlist new club members with much more confidence than the average father. And twins reinforced the claim that, "There's always room for one more in a VW."

Few promotions have captured the spirit and independence of a brand like this did for the fun VW. While it probably did not directly sell any "Bugs," it sure helped to establish an attitude in car buyers' minds. Especially if they're named Ricky VW Rayfield, Andrea Ghia Scholtz, or Arthur Vernon Walters.

Dr. Pepper—Picnic at the World's Fair Sweepstakes

Dr. Pepper's promotion strategy was built around "kookie contests" and this one was right on strategy. Dr. Pepper got in on the excitement of the day when in 1964 the company offered a picnic to visit the World's Fair in New York. Dr. Pepper spiced up the prize by making the visit a picnic with 50 of your friends. To make it even more appealing to young adults, prime Dr. Pepper drinkers, Dick Clark and a new starlet from *Muscle Beach Party* were added to host the event.

These kookie promotions worked well to extend Dr. Pepper's budget and recognition. Teens especially were looking for the outlandish and got very excited about these "distinctively different" promotions and about the soft drink. Who else but teens would appreciate the prize structure. Lower level prizes creatively carried out the picnic theme by offering paper napkins (with picnic baskets) and ant villages. (See Exhibit 2.3.)

General Electric— Slicing Knife Refund

Refunds were in their infancy in 1966 when GE offered $2.00 back on any of its automatic slicing knives. Small household appliances were the first category to offer refunds—and once started, all appliance manufacturers jumped on the bandwagon.

Offering to mail back part of the purchase price was a good way to offer a purchase incentive to customers at point of sale. Manufacturers expected slippage (customers not sending in for the offer) so they could afford to make a high value offer that helped sell the product at point of sale. And in the new discount stores of the '60s, salespeople who recommended products were no longer on the floor actually selling. So manufacturers had to depend on their products, packaging and promotions to sell the brands. And refunds were easy to understand, easy to execute for the retailer, and a value to consumers. (See Exhibit 2.4.)

First National City Travelers Checks—Trial Offer

While First National City Travelers Checks had been around for 63 years, in 1967 the company chose to "sample" its product to broaden its customer base. Competition in Travelers Checks was mounting with some heavy names—American Express and Diners Club—taking charge.

The offer was simple—up to $5,000 in Travelers Checks for only a $2.00 service fee during the month of May. And the promotion ad encouraged readers to buy during the promotion for upcoming summer vacations or business travel. The

EXHIBIT 2.3

EXHIBIT 2.4

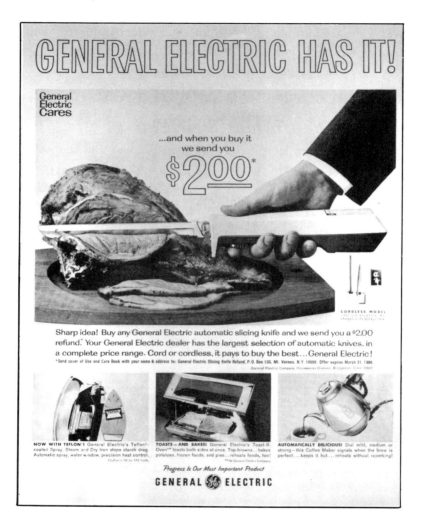

company wanted customers to "load their pantries" before competitive bank services offered summer promotions. This was a great example of the financial services industry using traditional package goods tactics and thinking! (See Exhibit 2.5.)

Dial Soap—Instant Sweepstakes

Few products can legitimately send customers into the shower to participate in a sweepstakes. But this underwater step made a lot of sense for Dial Soap. Game pieces inserted in magazines were printed with water soluble ink. When you took your piece into your shower and ran it under water, you found out instantly if you were a winner.

The '60s gave us many match and win sweepstakes where we took game pieces to match products or displays. But this game where you took your game piece with you to the showers could really add some excitement to your morning! The fun and involvement helped Dial Soap stand out from the rest. (See Exhibit 2.6.)

Oneida Tableware—Spoon Offer

Oneida and the other silver manufacturers have been offering starter spoons for years. We've seen this offer on Betty Crocker cake mix boxes and in bride's books forever. What caught our attention in this promotion ad is the sexy, sultry delivery.

The late '60s (this ad ran in 1967) saw the "love generation" come to marketing. We saw plenty of suggestive lips, knowing glances from behind long teasing blond bangs, and flirting poses in ads for free premiums or magazine subscriptions.

This ad delivers much more than an offer for a spoon. It seems to be promising romance and rendezvous in the copy. This was the '60s way of selling spoons. (See Exhibit 2.7.)

EXHIBIT 2.5

EXHIBIT 2.6

EXHIBIT 2.7

Premiums—Send Two Labels and 50¢

The explosion of new brands in the '60s brought forth an onslaught of creative promotions. Among the popular tactics were premiums—those free or inexpensive gifts, on-in-or near the package or offered through the mail with proofs of purchase.

While premiums and branded merchandise have been popular since the early days of Mr. Peanut and Cracker Jack, we're offering a look at some of the more effective recent premiums to demonstrate how they can help build brands.

Premiums for Loyalty

Premiums delivered in the supermarket offered a competitive advantage right at point-of-sale. In-pack glasses, towels, and silverware were commonly offered as gifts in powdered laundry detergents as a method to keep brand loyalty. These continuity efforts made brand decisions easy. Just look for the package with the Golden Leaf glass pattern (Silver Dust) until your glassware set is complete. Or choose Ivory Flakes for the bath towels instead. (See Exhibit 2.8.)

Other brands chose to make the offer on the package or at store displays as a way to draw attention and sales to the brand. Kraft offered women's nylons and then panty hose on the back panel of Parkay margarine for almost 25 years. They had women as loyal to their Powers Model Panty Hose as to their quality margarine. While hardly a premium that reinforced the brand usage, the offer of hosiery was very compelling to the audience.

Texaco supported its Fire Chief and Sky Chief gasolines with a children's fire chief helmet—an actual replica of those worn for real fire fighting. The history of this 1964 premium went back to 1932 when Ed Wynn, the comedian, began as a fire-fighting spokesman. Parents could keep the fire chief image alive with this $3.99 premium. (See Exhibit 2.9.)

EXHIBIT 2.8. Detergents could keep customers for years by offering collectible glassware, dishes or towels right in the package. Reprinted with permission.

EXHIBIT 2.9 Texaco's Fire Chief spokesman came to life with this children's premium. Reprinted with permission.

Premiums for Image

Virginia Slims has always led the pack on premiums that help extend and reinforce their brand image. Consider the annual Book of Days Engagement Calendar that serves as a yearlong collection of stories and ads that dimensionalize, "You've Come a Long Way, Baby."

The Virginia Slims Little Black Book telephone book was a natural to spoof the classic male/female roles. When rugby and jogging became popular male sports, Virginia Slims was at the forefront, offering delightfully chic versions for women. (See Exhibit 2.10.)

In the same Philip Morris family, we have seen the Marlboro authentic sheepskin coat, flannel shirts, trail dusters, and spurs be offered to bring a sharper focus to our already well-developed image of the Marlboro Man. Free premiums are never just key chains but are "Longhorn Star" keychains, complete with story.

Benson & Hedges, another PM family member, successfully reinforced an image of urban good taste by offering a series of very contemporary recipe books, each themed to the aspirations of the target market. The very best restaurants, the most luxurious resorts, the most romantic country inns all were brought to life for B&H smokers. (See Exhibit 2.11.)

Premiums for Fun and Long Term Loyalty

The folks at Pillsbury have always been blessed with wonderful ready-made premiums in their stable of characters. We have the Doughboy, recently brought back slightly hipper but just as lovable as ever. He has been offered in overstuffed cloth and roly-poly plastic and is now a theme for kitchen accessories. He has been introduced to children long before they are baking or making purchase decisions. He will continue to be a positive influence for the cooks of tomorrow.

Even more merchandised have been the wonderful cast of characters from the Valley—the Jolly Green Giant, Little Sprout, and

EXHIBIT 2.10 Each year Virginia Slims brings the slogan
"You've Come a Long Way, Baby" to life in a cleverly designed
engagement book. Reprinted with permission.

EXHIBIT 2.11 Benson & Hedges delivered urban good taste with a series of beautiful on-carton recipe books. Reprinted with permission.

all the other pixie-like workers. Pillsbury is not just selling vegetables with these guys. Instead we have a very memorable and fun oversized world with Green Giant merchandise. Some premiums you could mail for have been a monstrously huge umbrella, a large green footprint rug, and a child's chair in the shape (and size) of the Giant's hand. What child can't be charmed by the storybook thrill of a giant living in the pantry? (See Exhibit 2.12.)

When Little Sprout was brought to the Valley, he was introduced to America in the same fashion. Some of the most lasting premiums of Sprout have been a Little Sprout talking alarm clock, a Sprout telephone, a Sprout touch lamp and a cheery Sprout bank. Pillsbury has brought their symbol of product quality into children's rooms everywhere and made friends with tomorrow's decision makers.

Kodak film introduced its own species of colorful critters in 1989—Kolorkins. They made great children's toys and gave consumers a compelling reason to keep buying Kodak film to collect them all. (See Exhibit 2.13.)

These premiums cannot fail to help establish brand equity. And they probably got great display support from retailers with these clever gifts.

Premiums for Traffic

Movie theaters were the kings of traffic-building premiums in the 1930s. But it was gas stations and supermarkets who kept the tradition alive as a way to keep customers coming back. Gas station premium wars heated up as station owners called a truce on price wars. Drivers could choose from collecting sets of glasses, silverware, collectible sports coins, kitchen utensils. Like brand loyalty bought with detergent towel sets, America would select the housewares patterns to collect and stay loyal until the set was complete. (See Exhibit 2.14.)

Supermarkets were in the same premium mode with a different piece of china or silverplate offered each week. And what worked with traditional retailers was borrowed by the quick service restau-

EXHIBIT 2.12 Green Giant and Little Sprout have gone far beyond kitchens into children's rooms as the focus of many delightful premiums. Reprinted with permission.

EXHIBIT 2.13 Kodak's Kolorkins now join Little Sprout and other branded characters in kids' rooms. Reprinted courtesy Eastman Kodak Company.

EXHIBIT 2.14 Retailers from gas stations to theaters to quick service restaurants have offered glasses to keep customers coming back to build the set. Reprinted with permission.

rants as a way to build excitement and traffic for their hamburger/
beef/pizza/chicken/taco shops. Movie properties seem to be the
hottest tie-in with glasses or plastic cups being a solid premium.

Lessons from the Sixties

We owe many of today's promotion techniques to advances
made in the '60s. Some of them that live on are:

- Bonus pack and special premium packs came into vogue.
  Huge, modern supermarkets offered lots of shelf space for
  special packs. And retailers were happy to pass on extra
  savings or products to entice customers to buy more.
- Display-driven promotions brought a focus to retail. Match
  and win sweepstakes sent ad readers to stores to see if they
  had won. Displays carried samples of premiums as dealer
  loaders. And manufacturers put money into display contests to get more action at retail.
- Super brands were introduced, especially from Procter &
  Gamble, Lever Brothers, and Colgate-Palmolive. Money
  was available for whatever was necessary, so new products
  were introduced with huge media and sampling budgets.
- Co-op advertising helped manufacturers and retailers get more
  for their advertising dollars as retailers ventured into broadcast
  advertising as well as traditional newspapers/advertising.

We're in a very interesting phase in promotion. On one hand
we have the meteoric advances of promotion understanding and
consumer intelligence brought about by scanners and database
management. Then on the other hand we see the 1989 success of
Batman glasses at Taco Bell—over 4 million given away—and we
realize that's the same type of premium promotion America used
to court movie goers on Saturday afternoons in the 1930s. It surely
shows how human nature doesn't change . . . .

CHAPTER THREE

The Seventies—
Recession Hits

Oil. Those three letters were responsible for sending America into unbridled inflation, accompanied by the first real recession since before World War II.

From October 1973 until mid-March 1974 Arab oil-producing nations banned oil exports to the U.S. in an effort to put pressure on Israeli troops to withdraw from the Middle East. America had become totally dependent on oil and petroleum to power our cars, heat our homes, make plastics and materials, and keep America running. The immediate shortage from the oil embargo meant skyrocketing prices on the gas that was available and those prices never came down.

For the first time since World War II gas rationing stamps were printed. Though never used, they symbolized the lines at service stations and the panic gas buying that was the topic of conversation all winter long.

We were encouraged to carpool and plan shopping trips. Suddenly "one-stop shopping" was not just convenient but downright patriotic. Shopping malls and combination grocery/drug/ discount stores hopped on the bandwagon to encourage consumers to make one trip for all holiday needs in 1973.

If households weren't affected by gas station lines and winter energy saving tips, they could very well have been affected by unemployment. There simply was less money spent in the U.S. as more and more was being sent overseas to the oil-producing nations. That meant less development, and less employment.

And the short supply, higher priced oil meant price increases on any petroleum based products—plastics, gym shoes, machinery, building products, everything was touched by the price increases. Manufacturers and retailers learned to cut back on inventories in hopes that prices may come down. And they passed all their increases on to consumers, who also thought that sooner or later prices would have to come down. They never did.

All told, inflation rose the consumer price index to 161 in 1975 from just 100 in 1967.

The oil crisis also woke us up to the need for more energy-efficient cars. Unfortunately Detroit was slow to react and didn't downscale car sizes until after imports had taken over 20 percent of the auto business.

But then came America's Bicentennial and happier days as we turned our sights on the tall ships and the fireworks of the century. Between the Montreal Olympics and Mark Spitz, the start of video games and the fireworks, the mood of America started to look up. Government's WIN (Whip Inflation Now) efforts were well-meaning but did little to change fortunes except for button manufacturers. We were simply getting used to living with inflation.

EXHIBIT 3.1 Retailers stressed energy-saving "one-stop shopping" after the 1973 oil embargo. The convenience and number of Jewel-Osco combination food and drug stores made a compelling energy story for the Chicago market. Reprinted with permission.

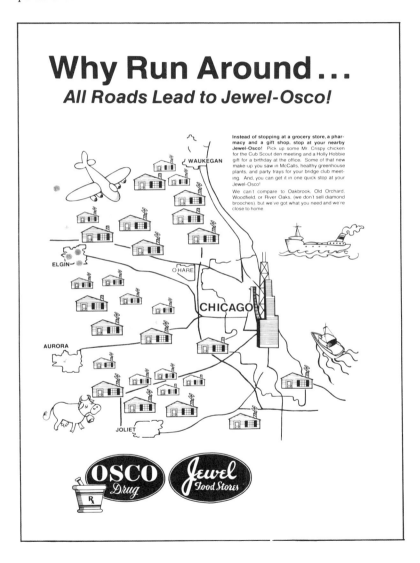

EXHIBIT 3.2 Recessionary times helped fuel the growth of credit cards. Master Charge was one of the leaders that promised America easy credit access. Reprinted with permission.

**Destination: Almost anywhere in the world.
With a Master Charge Card, you can leave today.**

Wisconsin Master Charge

Facts from the Seventies

■ 1970 brought a ban on broadcast advertising for cigarettes.

■ According to *Progressive Grocer*, in 1971 manufacturers' allowances to supermarkets reached $500,000,000 plus, equal to over $10,000 per supermarket.

■ The '70s brought talk of personal computers and the lifestyle revolution they would bring. Instead, in 1977 when the Apple II was introduced, it was mostly bought by hobbyists who talked programming to each other.

■ Watergate, the 26-month debacle of cover-ups and political wrongdoing, captured headlines from June 1972 through President Nixon's resignation on August 9, 1974. America will never look at Washington in the same way again.

■ "Light" became the magic word with beer; "diet" was the thing in soft drinks; and everything was becoming more "natural."

■ California and New York got into the wine action and significantly increased consumption of wines with corks.

■ Winnie the Pooh, with the promotion support of Sears, made a short-lived bid for the 1976 Presidential election.

■ In 1977, a bold Freddie Laker offered airfare to London for only $259. His Laker Airline stalled in profits when the big guys got worried.

■ 1978 danced to disco with Saturday Night Fever.

Signs of the Times—A Seventies Sampler of Promotions

We're still living with some of the promotional baggage we took on in the '70s. The auto industry started rebates as a way to move inventory. Packaged goods manufacturers contributed more heavily than ever to retail deals. And the FSI came into being to offer a simple, more cost-efficient promotion and couponing vehicle.

Hiring MBAs came into vogue in the late '70s. And with that bent, risk as a key element of marketing took a back seat as risk is not a subject for business schools.

By the end of the decade, sales promotion had been recognized by the communications industry and a few advertising agencies—Young & Rubicam; Foote, Cone, & Belding; Darcy—had begun their own capabilities. While initially these may have been set up as design and collateral arms for the agencies, many grew into full service promotion agencies.

Direct mail and the concept of pinpointing your target market became a reality as data management became easier and more commonplace with advanced technology.

A lot of terrific promotions were introduced in the '70s, too. We saw value added programs become the differentiating point for many brands. And we saw service industries start to promote like never before—a trend that continues to grow today.

Hunt-Wesson—Menu Plan 2

The headline of this promotional ad sums up the economic situation of the early '70s very well. "If living on your food budget is no easier this month than it was last month." Hunt's offer got right to the point—send the coupon indicating your family size and weekly food budget and Hunt-Wesson would send you back a computerized monthly meal plan with nutritionally balanced menus and recipes.

What a smart way to get recipes that called for Hunt-Wesson products into the home. And what a helpful gesture to those struggling in a tough economy. (See Exhibit 3.3.)

Toyota—Olympics Viewing Guide

While the Olympics may have reached their exposure limit in the '80s, TV sponsorship in the '70s had opened doors for promotions. Toyota used their Summer Olympics sponsorship to

EXHIBIT 3.3

offer a free television viewing guide as a traffic builder for dealer showrooms. (See Exhibit 3.4.)

Campbell's Soup—
Labels for Education

Begun in 1973 when school budgets were being cut and important education programs were eliminated from government support, Campbell's has since donated over $40 million to local schools and libraries.

The "cause" offer is simple. Schools collect labels from Campbell's Soups and other Campbell's owned brands. At the end of the collection year, they turn the labels in for selected audio-visual, sports, computer, and other school equipment.

One of the first "Frequent Eater" programs, it couldn't be more perfect for rewarding heavy users in a meaningful way— with quality education equipment. The cause works, the mechanics work, and the Campbell's Kids work creatively in the classroom setting. (See Exhibit 3.5.)

Cessna Aircraft—
Trial Flight Coupon

Cessna got a lot of word-of-mouth attention from this coupon promotion because it made "test flying" an airplane so easy. The offer was a flight lesson demonstration in a Cessna, with an instructor, and you get to take the controls . . . all for only $5.00. You even take home an official Pilot Flight Log with your minutes at the controls recorded.

Cessna's promotional approach is right on track—grow the market of potential users for your product. Because more people flying small planes means more people to buy Cessna. (See Exhibit 3.6.)

EXHIBIT 3.4

EXHIBIT 3.5

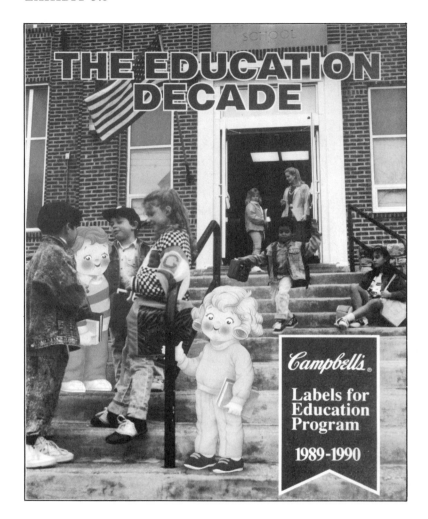

EXHIBIT 3.6

Nabisco—"Horton Hears a Who" Sponsorship and Premium

What could be a better tie-in than cookies and Dr. Seuss? Nabisco cleverly sponsored the telecast of this popular children's book, then supported their sponsorship with a premium offer. For two cookie labels and $1.00, you could receive the $2.95 book by mail. Best of all, the entire promotion ad was in Dr. Seuss–like rhyme for a real creative coup. (See Exhibit 3.7.)

Standard Oil— Tire Tread Tester

Here's an offer that Standard cannot afford to make any more! Buy four tires and get 50 gallons of gas free! This 1971 promotion hardly foresaw the gas shortages and energy crisis that was to follow in 1973. While gas wars were common, it was necessary for service stations to make their money on ancillary products. So in the early '70s we saw a glut of oil offers and tire deals. Standard's offer was especially effective with the tipped in Tread Tester that lets you see for yourself if your tires had reached a dangerous level of wear. (See Exhibits 3.8 and 3.9.)

The Value War against Generics

Jewel Food Stores in Chicago introduced a new concept in 1977 that helped force the promotion issue to the forefronts of supermarket shelves and customers' minds. They introduced generics—those plain white-wrapped products without cute names or fancy labels. Stenciled in brown across the front was simply the generic word for the product.

Generics were a brilliant concept for the time. Double digit inflation was causing frequent price increases on name brands. And for consumers during the recessionary times of the late '70s,

EXHIBIT 3.7

EXHIBIT 3.8

Tear out this tire tester.
It's worth 50 gallons of gasoline.
Maybe even your life.
How are your tires? Government safety studies show that dangerously worn tires are 10 times more likely to have a flat than new tires. And it's a fact that nearly one out of every three passenger cars on the road has at least one unsafe tire. So tear out this tire tester and check all your tires. If the tester shows they're dangerously worn, drive in to your nearby Standard Oil Dealer. Negotiate a deal with him. Get his best price. And on top of that, we'll give you 50 free gallons of gasoline with the purchase of 4 new ATLAS® tires. Or 25 free gallons with the purchase of two. You know they've got to be good—because when you buy a tire from us, we both live with it. See your participating Standard Oil Dealer today. The sooner the safer.
(In Wisconsin, see dealer's posted prices for tires.)
STANDARD
Standard Oil Division
American Oil Company

EXHIBIT 3.9

this lower cost, lower quality alternative was a new direction for budget relief. Pricing was about 30% less than brand names and 15% less than private label goods.

Generics quickly spread throughout the marketplace with paper products and ingredient-type items (cheese, oils) leading sales. Buying generics meant "shopping smart," especially among the discriminating college-educated shoppers who prided themselves on their generic selections.

And as the recession continued, generics kept building share until both their popularity and the recession peaked in 1982. Nearly $2.8 billion were spent that year on generics, capturing 2.4% of total share of supermarket sales, according to SAMI data.

Some categories were significantly stronger than others. Generic frozen food share hit 16.5%; nonfood dry grocery generics captured 13.1%. Even health and beauty aids, the weakest category for generics saw 7.3% of sales go to the plain wrappered products.

Branded Options

What could a branded product do if it was suddenly up against a "cheap rip-off" that was stealing share? There were a few options, each bearing a cost on bottom line profits.

- Some manufacturers differentiated their products by quality, making them significantly superior, so much so that the higher price was clearly justified. P&G went this route with Charmin and Bounty with ongoing advertising trumpeting the product claims. Others made their products look very different from the generics, as the pet food companies did by introducing soft, moist varieties and new flavors and shapes of dried food.
- Some manufacturers lowered prices significantly. A number of food manufacturers compromised on their healthy profits and were able to offer their products for less

money—not down to generic pricing levels, but to where customers recognized a better value.

- Some manufacturers made promotion work harder at retail. As marketers scrambled to add value to their brands with promotion, the promotion supplier status quo was challenged for breakthrough technology and ideas.
- New technology allowed in-pack games and sweepstakes like Hunt's "Hunt for the Gold" under-the-lid game and Cracker Jack's "Instant Surprise" game. New printing and application technology brought on-pack removeable labels for instant redeemable coupons. This compelling technique helped bring brand name products to the consumer's attention at the point of sale.
- New media including the free standing insert and new telephone technology helped deliver promotions with more potential for consumer involvement than ever before. Cap'n Crunch's "Find LaFoote" sweepstakes broke all telephone records and sales records while achieving involvement from a tough audience—children. (See Exhibit 3.10.)
- Refund and promotion values escalated as consumers were asked to save labels in return for high value cash refunds. Slippage was high so these offers were affordable. And to the consumer, they offered a value that compared well against generic pricing.
- Manufacturers started dealing even heavier with the trade, trying harder than ever to get ad and in-store price features.
- And some smart marketers recognized the importance of building their established brands and, rather than fighting generics on price, chose to add value to the purchase. So we saw more Marlboro Country Store premium offers that reinforced the Marlboro Man image. And we saw Del Monte bring their vegetable products to life with the "Country Yumkins." While generics and price brands were caught in a downward spiral, many well-established brands that withstood the price wars held on with the help of brand-building promotions.

EXHIBIT 3.10 Quaker Oats' "Find LaFoote" treasure hunt for Cap'n Crunch cereal built excitement, involvement and, ultimately, loyalty in a price-focused marketing arena for cereals. Reprinted with permission.

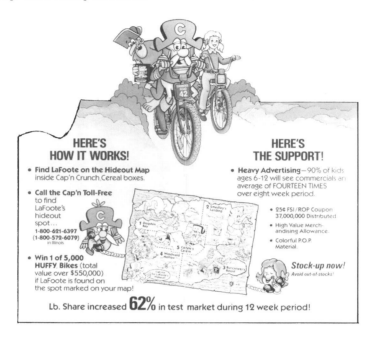

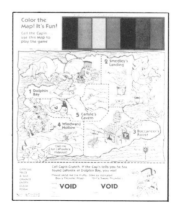

Brand Names WIN!

Today you'll still find a selection of generic products in the larger supermarkets but they are no longer the threat to the brand names that they had been. The upswing in the economy in the '80s pushed generics to the background. As salaries escalated and the unemployment situation grew brighter, most Americans went back to favorite brands. Yet the foray into generics made marketers pay attention to customers, their price/value acceptance, and the role of promotion in the marketplace.

Del Monte—The Case for Plush Vegetables

Scattered in children's bedrooms throughout America are the Del Monte Yumkins—cute, stuffed, smiling green peas, roly-poly red tomatoes, and every child's favorite—the carrot. From time to time, Del Monte freshens the vegetable patch with other farm-fresh selections, such as a comical stuffed crow and a matching scarecrow or a cuddly fluffy lamb. What had begun as a clever premium program has grown to be one of America's most successful continuity programs. (See Exhibit 3.11.)

The Del Monte Situation

In the late 1970s—partly as a result in the surge in generics—the canned fruits and vegetables category had turned into a promotion battleground. To differentiate branded goods, we saw a lot of promotion activity. Favored techniques were cents-off labels and high value, escalating refunds, which was Del Monte's standard approach. While initially successful, consumers were becoming immune to this overexposed tactic while the trade became blasé. Even more important was Del Monte's realization that their cash refund approach had actually hurt their brand image. Their price-focused strategy had established their products as commodities in consumers' minds.

Objectives
1. To generate high volume sales.
2. To generate massive displays.
3. To create consumer excitement and preference.
4. To help build long-term corporate and product image, positioning Del Monte as a warm, family-oriented company.

Strategies
1. Offer unique premiums that represent a good value, appeal to Moms and reinforce the product name and imagery.
2. Require huge quantities of purchase to receive the premiums for free.
3. Make premiums the focus of attention-getting displays.

The Winning Big Idea

Country Yumkins took the supermarkets by storm with product and Yumkin displays that won the hearts of America. These stuffed, plush vegetables and fruits were cute, different and high value. And they were totally identified with Del Monte and the image they were trying to establish.

Initially, customers could get a free Yumkin with only 50 labels or five labels and $8.95. Later the stakes were raised so you could *only* get Country Yumkins with 75 proofs of Del Monte purchase and response stayed just as strong.

The Results

The first year was such a hit the Country Yumkin program was immediately scheduled for future years with new Yumkins making their way on to the Del Monte farm. In the first three

EXHIBIT 3.11 Del Monte Country Yumkins® plush toy was a clever value-added promotion that replaced cents-off labels and refunds with memorable premiums. The promotion was exceptionally effective against inexpensive generic canned goods. Reprinted with permission.

years, 1.5 million Country Yumkins were ordered by more than one million consumers, about 70 percent of whom sent in all 50 or 75 labels.

Del Monte recognized the continued success of the Country Yumkin promotion. As Steve Rothschild, V.P. of Marketing at Del Monte when the Yumkins program started, said, ''As a rule, I oppose running the same promotion year after year. But Country Yumkins was such a success, we would have been nuts to walk away from it.''

Country Yumkins is over ten years old and continues to be a sure-fire success in getting attention at retail and getting Del Monte products into consumers' homes. In 1990, 80 labels and a $2.00 handling charge will get you Sweetie Pea or Cobbie Corn.

The Best Annual Events

''We'll do it again this year because it worked last year.''

These are the words that make those of us in the business of creating promotions cringe! Said by a client, it comes as a verbal dare to come up with something better. In most cases, it's easy to best previous promotions with a better offer, a new creative idea, or a stronger, more contemporary strategy. But as was the case with Del Monte's Yumkins and the following promotions, some events actually get stronger when run year after year. Each rerun may mean new twists or tactical improvements, but the basic theme and ideas stay the same.

So here we salute the perennials in which smart marketers have seen the value to ''doing it again this year.''

''Pick a Pair'' from Budweiser began in 1957 and continues as an annual multiple purchase sales event. The theme works so well and been so ingrained through advertising and display that America expects this themed sales every summer. Bud's newest annual event ties in with the Super Bowl. The ''Bud Bowl'' pits Bud against Bud Light. The promotion starts at point of sale and reaches its climax during the commercials that play the "Bud Bowl" game. We look forward to this exciting event to spice up the Super Bowl in years to come!

"Kraft Salad Days" offers retailers a three-month produce event and gives customers even more reasons to buy Kraft products. Since 1970, Kraft has been bringing together produce suppliers like Dole and the California Avocado Advisory Board under the promotional banner of "Kraft Salad Days." Supermarkets love it as Kraft provides an event to promote, great point of sale items, and special prices on their dressings and salad fixings. Consumers appreciate the recipes for new in-season salad ideas and great savings on the fresh ingredients. And the visibility of Kraft's products within stores reaches an annual high.

"Marlboro Country Store" collection of image-enhancing self-liquidating premiums has captured smokers' imaginations and two promotion industry Robbie Awards since 1972. Each premium is chosen for its authenticity and ability to extend Marlboro Country on our minds. The marketers at Philip Morris keep this program in perspective—they never worry about how many premiums they'll sell. They worry about how the premiums contribute to Marlboro's single-focused image. And that's why the Country Store concept stays so strong.

Super Bowl promotions have become such an annual event that you'd expect Hallmark to have cards for the occasion. For the trade, the football theme makes sense. But do football helmet snack bowls, football-shaped telephones and NFL sweatshirts really appeal to Mom, the family shopper? But we applaud Budweiser for the Bud Bowl—a *real* Super Bowl promotion that gets involvement from beer drinkers—and everyone who cares about the game.

We were happy to see some old time favorites recently return. Some of these are:

- The Nestle's Quick Bunny Cup with handles shaped like the bunny's ears. Chocolate milk is always more fun when served in a character mug!
- "Be the Breck Girl." While lots of cosmetic companies

EXHIBIT 3.12 (a)–(d) ''Pick a Pair'' from Budweiser has been an annual feature of summer in American stores since 1957. Reprinted with permission.

(a) "Pick a Pair"—1960

(b) "Pick a Pair"—1963

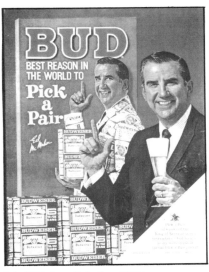

(c) "Pick a Pair"—1967

(d) "Pick a Pair"—1971

EXHIBIT 3.13 "Kraft Salad Days" offered retailers an event they could promote with point of sale, recipes and savings throughout the store. Kraft is a registered trademark of Kraft General Foods, Inc. Reprinted with permission.

EXHIBIT 3.14 The Marlboro Country Store concept remains strong today, still contributing to Marlboro's focused image. Reprinted with permission.

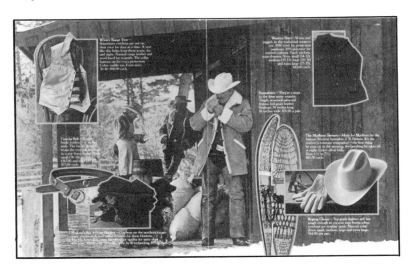

EXHIBIT 3.15 Annual NFL promotions succeed in grocery stores because of trade support, not from consumer interest. Reprinted with permission.

EXHIBIT 3.16 Budweiser's "Bud Bowl" event is right on target for beer drinkers. Reprinted with permission.

have looked for models and cover girls, few marketers have been able to position their product as succinctly as Breck Shampoo. This contest looks for the clean, conservative girl in the ads—like the shampoo, no extravagance, no brash fashion statements.

- ''The Pepsi Challenge.'' This promotion seems to show up at special events and as a welcome street corner sampling activity on summer days. We love the focus on product and credibility!

Let's bring back the good ones!

Promoting Yourself and Your Business

Let me start by telling you I never did a marketing or promotion plan for myself or my business. Like many other entrepreneurs, I was too busy doing/selling/collecting to take the time to plan. But my ''notoriety'' in this industry and the subsequent promotion of myself and the agency comes from a sincere drive to have this great business of sales promotion become more professional and recognized as such. I just saw some opportunities along the way and capitalized on them.

Let me share some things I learned that may help you do this difficult task of promoting yourself and your business to build your future.

After the agency was relatively established, we looked around and realized that advertising had its David Ogilvys and Leo Burnetts, direct mail had its Stones and Adlers, marketing had its Stuart Henderson Britts and Peter Druckers, but who was speaking out about sales promotion? No one. So some of my staff and I started writing articles on good and bad promotions that we saw and submitted them to the trade journals of the day. That led to a regular column in *Advertising Age*, ''Robinson on Promotion.''

The success of the column and the rise in interest in sales promotion led to speaking engagements at workshops and college classes; then client seminars and lectures; and eventually a public seminar in 1985. In the meantime, Don Schultz from Northwestern University and I finally put down on paper what sales promotion is all about in a series of books that are still required college reading today.

In 1973 we looked around the industry again and saw that, once again, advertising, direct mail, public relations, and marketing all had their annual awards. So we captured that opportunity and created the Best Promotions of the Year awards. In 1986, we named them the ''Robbies'' after my father who had been a copywriter, and added the eagle statuettes. (See Exhibit 3.17.)

The most important aspect of these activities is that they require a significant commitment in time and effort. Some of these were opportunities open only in the early stages of the business. But they proved to be critical in developing the agency and I thought they may shed some light for any entrepreneurs reading this book.

In a nutshell, here are my thoughts on using promotion and self-promotion to build a business:

1. Do a plan. Start out with some good ideas, prioritize them, find out what needs to be done to execute them and *set up a time line*. You may have the most exciting idea or news in the world, but until you set a schedule to tell the world, no one will ever know about it.
2. Get published. This starts with a good idea or a strong viewpoint that will capture readers' attention. You can query magazines or newspapers first for submission requirements. Or start with a Letter to the Editor or a letter to a personal opinion column.
3. Keep submitting material. Call the publisher with a good feature idea. Send editors notes on their work with your feedback.
4. Use your published material to promote your business.

EXHIBIT 3.17 The eagle statuette given to ROBBIE Award winners is proudly displayed by some of the best marketers in America.

Arrange for reprints and mail them to your clients, potential clients and former clients. This gives you a credible reason to stay top-of-mind.

5. Offer to speak at local organizations or national meetings. While these take a lot of planning time and money, they can be extremely rewarding in contacts and shared ideas. But please, have something important to say if you're going to offer your expertise.

6. Follow up with every media inquiry. Learn the hierarchy of your local business press and follow etiquette. And always answer calls from the media.

7. Keep in mind that the public doesn't want to hear about you. However, they do want to hear your new ideas, new technology, or new breakthrough thinking. And if they learn your name and something about you along the way, so much the better.

Promoting your own business and yourself should not be pushed to the bottom of your to-do list but deserves regular attention and effort. Keep with it and keep looking for those opportunities.

Lessons from the Seventies

Plenty of the advances from the '70s are with us today:

- Free Standing Inserts (FSIs). Though introduced in 1972, it took until 1982 for FSIs to become the dominant medium for delivering coupons. By 1989, FSIs accounted for over 80 percent of coupons distributed.
- In-pack sweepstakes, from Cracker Jack and beyond, finally overcame the "No purchase necessary" legal restrictions.
- Thematic promotions, whether based on breakfast or tied to Thanksgiving dinner. Thematics originated in the early

'70s as co-op ventures, based on the premise that tying related brands together makes more media and cost impact. In the '90s tie-ins are more prolific than ever before!

• Auto rebates—unfortunately. Does anyone have an idea of what American cars really cost? They've been rebated for so long, the fire-sale rebates introduced for clearing out inventory have destroyed the price/value relationship for domestic autos.

CHAPTER FOUR

The Eighties—
Warfare in a
Time of Peace

Let's think about the military in the 1980s for a minute. We saw a few skirmishes in the Falklands. And a flash attack in Grenada. And truly unsettling hostage and terrorism situations in the Mid-East. But America was not ''at war'' overseas in this decade.

Instead the wars were happening at home. And not the civil unrest of the civil rights movement or students of the '60s. Instead war was waged on Wall Street with leveraged buyouts. It was waged among MBA graduate Yuppies fighting for condo turf and BMW tanks. It was the private sector supporting favorite public sector projects so that homelessness was an issue but poverty and the shrinking middle class weren't. Towards the end of the decade, as America moved to ''a kinder and gentler nation,'' we chose to fight big business and the Exxons of the world who were taking away our ecological future. And we questioned the credibility of America's business as Japan's manufacturing and financial strengths started to be felt throughout the States.

Marketing Warfare

Nowhere did the battles rage more noisily than in the marketing community. Beginning with Trout and Reis' bestseller on positioning and marketing strategy, *Marketing Warfare*, the sound of war raged. Let's look at some of the '80s skirmishes.

Share Wars

Out of the ''Buy all you want, we'll make more'' '60s, beyond the inflationary '70s, America moved into an economy of deregulation and competition. Airlines, telecommunications, and transportation all were opened to competition. We saw People's Express and Laker Airlines start and end. And we saw the end to Ozark, Piedmont, and, more than once, Braniff Airlines as Chapter 11 proceedings or reorganizations disrupted schedules. New long distance telephone companies arose to add competition to America's telephone company, AT&T. While deregulation improved prices and generally contributed to significant growth in each of the deregulated categories, the messages to consumers often came as switching messages. ''You'll save more with Sprint,'' ''MCI saves you more,'' etc., with each telecommunications company doing their math slightly differently to make that competitive claim.

American Airlines introduced their AAdvantage program as a way to lock in their profitable business travelers and lock out other competitive airlines. And the other airlines, hotels and car rental companies followed suit, forming strategic alliances with the various airlines as they lined up for Frequent Flyer Wars.

In grocery stores, we saw many categories maturing and moving into share showdowns. The decade started with Cookie Wars in Kansas City with P&G's Duncan Hines brand leading the soft, chewy packaged cookie introduction, quickly followed by Grandma's Cookies from Frito-Lay and then Soft Batch from Keebler. Live samples were delivered to doorsteps. Free package coupons were run weekly in newspapers. Sampling events were held at every mall and school event. Packaged cookie consumption rose by 27% in Kansas City just from the noise. And then came Mrs. Fields . . . .

But in cookie wars we saw the start of the marketing warfare that Coke and Pepsi, Burger King and McDonald's, Chrysler and the imports were to wage in this decade. Basically, consumption was at top levels for each of these categories. Except for adding Coke for Breakfast and Pepsi AM, we were full of soft drinks. And at the maximum in our "share of tummy" with quick service restaurants, we looked to promotional warfare to make us turn right into Burger King rather than left for McDonald's. The economy was such that we weren't buying cars like we used to . . . but demanding better quality and paying for it when we did purchase or rent.

The War Is in the Stores

Slotting allowances was the ammo that retailers introduced against manufacturers in the new product introduction wars. If you wanted to see your product sold in our stores, pay $4,000 per store ransom. And manufacturers paid it—and still are paying.

Once in-store, ActMedia assaulted consumers with paid point-of-sale (POS). Once retailers won the skirmish of who controls POS, manufacturers resorted to the old-time cigarette merchandising method of paying for POS. Only it was nicely

EXHIBIT 4.1 Grandma's® brand Cookies from Frito-Lay used a coupon sweepstakes as part of their arsenal in cookie wars in the early '80s. Reprinted with permission.

coordinated with national distribution and quality 4-color printing through ActMedia. It was this innovative POS group that claimed in its advertising ''The War Is in the Stores'' and then set out the rest of the ammunition to help win. Shopping cart ads, POP radio, ActNow sampling and coupon distribution, shelf talkers, and take-one pads guaranteed to exclusively support your product were the tactics.

Clearly ActMedia recognized the importance of the in-store decision in sales and capitalized on this. Today's research shows that most categories will see significant gains when POS calls attention to it in-store. And that advertising impressions are more meaningful in-store than in the comfort of the home. With ActMedia's category exclusivity, you would buy share of mind for your products in store. A powerful strategy.

Guerilla Couponing

We talk of scattershot targeting versus sharpshooting in delivering promotional offers. The old days of targeting everyone (scattershot) worked well when products were new, unique and filled a need. The '80s brought segmentation and specific positionings to meet America's niches, and the need for marketers to be very good sharpshooters. The media became more targeted as we saw a proliferation of special interest magazines and cable television shows. And our promotional vehicles, especially database management and direct mail, brought us closer to the important people we need to impact for product success.

Going after the competition was critical at this stage of the share wars. We saw the ''pit bull tactics'' of Catalina's Coupon Solution that delivered high value coupons to competitive users and low value repurchase coupons to current users at the scanner checkout lanes in stores. And guerilla tactics grew with the product usage databases from Computerized Technologies and other information sources that had the names and purchase habits of more than 20 million households.

Ambush Tactics in Special Events

The '80s saw the rise in sponsorship and special events as promotion vehicles and loyalty building opportunities. Jōvan started the decade with the first commercial sponsorship of a rock tour, the Rolling Stones 1981 American Tour. (See Exhibit 4.2.) Then came Live Aid, the Statue of Liberty, and the Olympics. And more Super Bowl hype than ever before. With all these sponsorships came ambush tactics that showed real creativity in marketing.

For example, Kodak was the official film of the LA Olympics. So Fuji took a different tact and bought all the billboards around the stadiums. By offering game-related premiums, Fuji basically confused the consumer into thinking it, not Kodak, was the big time sponsor. Similarly, we saw huge numbers of Lady Liberty knock-offs by non-official sponsors who simply borrowed the halo of patriotism and excitement to bring interest to their brands. (See Exhibit 4.3.)

The most recent ambush tactics have focused on the beer company sponsorships. While Miller paid dearly for the Who Reunion Tour, it was Budweiser who bought the sponsorship of the HBO television special. Bud promoted the Special as though it owned the whole tour. And most of the target audience came to think Bud *did* own the tour. Very creative.

Corporate Takeovers

Nowhere has the fighting been more bloody than in the boardrooms of big business. In the '80s new records were being set monthly for bigger buyouts and megamergers. Once the mergers took place, the fallout of excess debt and people took their tolls. Duplicate departments in marketing, personnel, finance, etc. saw big layoffs. Consolidation of marketing agencies and media buying hit. And, most importantly, was an even stronger focus on fast profits and short-term thinking. These companies needed to pay for their acquisitions when the bonds came due. So brand building activities seemed to go by the wayside and

EXHIBIT 4.2 Jōvan offered the first rock tour sponsorship in 1981, complete with tour posters as premiums. Reprinted with permission.

EXHIBIT 4.3 Coke scored big by bringing together America's most touching causes—saving the Statue of Liberty and "adopting" Cabbage Patch dolls. Reprinted with permission.

dollars were quickly focused on buying business as fast as possible.

In one sense, this goal was critical in moving sales promotion ahead in the ranks of the communication world. But the short-term focus caused some irreparable damage to some of America's most trusted brands. Winston cigarettes now relies heavily on coupons to keep its franchise. Pepsodent and Post cereals are fighting for survival. Detroit has sadly entrenched itself in rebate wars. As Ford has shown, the only way out is to offer quality products.

The Good Side of War

Along with all the casualties of war came some very exciting positive advances. The marketing warfare of the '80s has brought about entirely new categories like the burgeoning microwave convenience foods and shelf stable foods. We now have superior product packaging in many areas in response to retailer requests for better shelf utilization. And real competition has resulted in real service improvements in the new deregulated companies.

So we got the good with the bad. And the sales promotion profession has grown as a result.

Facts from the Eighties

- The 1980 elections helped introduce 900 telephone numbers when ABC-TV invited Reagan-Carter debate viewers to decide the winner by telephone at 50¢ a call.
- 1980 was the beginning of designer jeans and Brooke Shields in her Calvins. Clothes labels have not been the same since.
- 1981 saw the first major sponsorship of a rock tour. Jōvan brought the Rolling Stones to two million fans in 45 cities.
- 1984 winners were hair mousses, ''Where's the Beef?'',

Swatch watches, and Mary Lou Retton at the Los Angeles Olympics.

■ 1985 brought us New Coke. While some critics called it "the biggest marketing fiasco since the Edsel," it drove category sales up off the charts.

■ The average supermarket opened in 1987 measured 46,892 square feet, almost 3-1/2 times the size of a 1953 supermarket.

■ Dry beers, low alcohol beers, wine coolers, and premixed, canned cocktails all debuted in the '80s, but none had the star power of light beer in the '70s.

Just the Facts, Ma'am— Couponing in the Eighties

Perhaps the quickest way to illustrate how promotion grew in the '80s is to look at the growth of couponing, particularly through the use of free standing inserts (FSIs). Simple numbers tell the story:

Coupons distributed	1980: 90.6 billion
	1989: 273.4 billion
	(over 3,000 per household)
Coupons redeemed	1980: 3.5 million (4%)
	1989: 7.1 billion (3%)
	(*Marketing Week*, March 5, 1990)
Average coupon value	1980: 19.8¢
	1989: 50¢
	(Nielsen Marketing Research)

Percentage of companies compiling a consumer database for future targeted promotions:

ALL—49%
Largest ($1 BIL +): 72%
Smallest (– $1 BIL): 36%
(Donnelly 10th Annual Survey)

While the numbers say growth, they call for an explanation. Why did couponing grow by over 2,000 coupons per household each year? What were the key trends in growth?

Rise of the Free Standing Insert

Although it was introduced by Valassis Printing in 1972, broad reach distribution of the free standing insert of over 30 million was hit in 1981. As newspapers signed on and circulation grew, FSIs became even more appealing to advertisers as a fast, powerful way to reach consumers. At the close of the decade, circulation topped 50 million, far more than the most popular magazines—*TV Guide* and *Reader's Digest* at 16–18 million.

Even more powerful than the distribution numbers was the fast consumer acceptance of this promotional media. As coupon offers ballooned and total FSI savings values grew to over $100 in some newspaper issues, homemakers intent on saving learned to look for Sunday's paper and the FSI sections. Today FSIs are one of the most well-read newspaper sections, reaching 60% of households in the top 300 markets. And 30% of households buy Sunday papers to receive coupon savings, according to a Product Movers' survey.

Coupons and promotions in general reached higher acceptance levels. While household use of coupons grew from 70% to 77% from 1980–88, we saw a significant increase in number of coupons aimed at targets we previously thought were not promotionally responsive.

Motor oil and men's hair care coupons began to appear in *Sports Illustrated* and *Playboy*. *Ebony* and *Essence* began carrying well-written ads with coupons and recipes reflecting ethnic heritage and tastes. More manufacturers went to local Hispanic newspapers to target coupons to this very brand-loyal segment. The latest target for promotion has been kids and teens, since Kraft was met with strong response to a targeted corporate program aimed at teenaged girls. (See Exhibit 4.4.)

EXHIBIT 4.4 Kraft found out how very strong teen brand loyalty could be when it ran this continuity program for its grocery products. Reprinted with permission.

Not Just for Packaged Goods Any More

One of the most exciting transitions in the promotion industry is the shift from a totally packaged goods product orientation to a rise in promotions by services and hard goods. And that led to some very interesting coupon events over the decade.

Chicagoland Chevy dealers ran an attention-getting ad with a coupon for cents off per pound on Chevy trucks, just like supermarkets. Citicorp delivered a truly valuable coupon travel book in 1981 to bank customers purchasing Travelers Checks.

MCI sampled their new long distance telephone service with a coupon in 1983 as telecommunications became the newest service to begin promoting. United led the way in couponing in the newly deregulated airline industry in 1981 as it offered current passengers half fare coupons for their next United flight in a positive move to fill planes after a pilot strike. (See Exhibit 4.5.)

Even many packaged companies that previously never couponed jumped on the bandwagon. The cigarette category moved from being one of the non-players in couponing to being one of the causes of clutter over the past decade. In response to the declining user-base and the need for trial and switching in the cigarette share wars, some manufacturers found media- and mail-delivered coupons to be the broad reach, cost-efficient trial vehicle needed.

Part of the proliferation of coupons can be blamed on "the trade." Because of the visibility and store level impact of a 52-million circulation FSI coupon, retailers expect a coupon in support of any promotional efforts, especially a new product introduction.

Double, and even triple, couponing has become a common retail promotion tactic in some markets as supermarketers are battling for traffic and loyalty at the expense of manufacturers' coupon redemption rates and liability.

Too Much of a Good Thing?

Some marketers have begun to question seriously the millions of dollars spent on coupons and have looked for ways to cut back

EXHIBIT 4.5 United Airlines borrowed a traditional packaged goods technique, the bounceback coupon, to build traffic after a 1981 strike. Reprinted with permission.

redemption without losing trade support. Oddly enough, one of the ways is to run even more coupons on a page. The premise is that more coupons will be more confusing and that you must cut through the low-interest brand coupons to reach the ones that all of America wants. It works. And it's contributing to coupon clutter.

Other manufacturers are running multiple coupons in ads to help build distribution of multiple flavors or sizes. While average coupon redemption may drop and original product sales may be cannibalized, overall redemption and sales to the trade will certainly increase. And the lucky consumer gets even more coupon choices!

New Methods of Coupon Distribution

While FSIs capture the lion's share of coupons, several companies are betting their livelihood on better targeted alternate delivery methods. We've seen a major increase in companies building their own databases as a way to talk directly with their own customers away from the clutter of other manufacturers. Targeted direct mail delivery, though costly and expected to get even more so, can be very efficient if marketers can use them to identify potential heavy users.

So we see databanks like Select 'n Save identifying product users and their potential for heavy usage. Then, using direct mail, they send back computerized coupons with values based on brand usage and purchase frequency.

Catalina Couponing turned to in-store delivery to offer coupons to buyers of competitive and complimentary products. For example, you might receive a high value Pepsi coupon if you buy Coke, or a top brand coupon if you regularly buy dog food.

Other distribution methods aren't nearly as technical. Instant-redeem coupons attached to the package rose in popularity in some categories so that every brand now carries a coupon. What had been created as a tactic to break parity at shelf level became a cost of doing business on some brands.

Another interesting phenomenon is coupons being distributed

EXHIBIT 4.6 Toys R Us recognized the value of their stores as a promotional medium in the late '80s and began offering samples and coupons in targeted ''R Treat'' packages. Reprinted with permission.

by other retailers and service operations. Now you can get coupons from your bank ATM machine in addition to getting cash. And Burger King offered coupons for Encyclopaedia Brittanica with a Whopper purchase. Video stores offer microwave popcorn coupons. And Toys R Us stores have become a coupon and sampling medium with their R Treat package. (See Exhibit 4.6.)

How Many Is Too Many?

In 1999 will we look back and smile at only 3,000 coupons delivered per family per year? Will we be seeing hospital coupons for 10% off any elective surgery or "Save $2,000 on Childbirth"? Or will paper coupons be a thing of the '80s, replaced by UPC codes, cards, and scanners?

The '80s saw volume growth and new and exciting delivery methods. Now we're looking at quality growth and better targeting.

Signs of the Times—An Eighties Sampler of Promotions

What a great time to be in this business! While computer capabilities opened doors to database management and allowed us to develop frequent flier programs, other consumer companies took equally giant leaps and invested millions of dollars into image-building, with some amazing promotions. Let's look at some of the '80s promotions that stand out.

American Airlines AAdvantage Program

In the first of the frequent flyer programs that changed our travel habits for the '80s, American found a very convincing way to

EXHIBIT 4.7

Our AAdvantage℠ program is a simple way for you to earn travel awards based on the mileage you fly. Here's how it works:

The more you fly, the greater the rewards.

Your travel awards depend on the amount of mileage you accumulate in any 12-month period. When you reach a mileage award level, you will have the option of redeeming that award *or* continuing on to the next level. Here's what you can earn:

Mileage	Your Travel Award
12,000	A First Class upgrade on any Coach round-trip ticket to anywhere American flies.
20,000	25% off a round-trip ticket to any American Airlines destination.
30,000	50% off a round-trip ticket to any American Airlines destination.
40,000	75% off a round-trip ticket to any American Airlines destination.
50,000	A free First Class round-trip ticket to any American Airlines destination, *plus* one First Class ticket upgrade for the companion of your choice.
75,000	Two First Class round-trip tickets to any American Airlines destination.

When you redeem your travel award, American Airlines will automatically send along to you certificates good for special bonus extras on car rentals and hotel discounts — compliments of Hertz Rent-A-Car and Hyatt Hotels.

Once you have accepted a travel award, your total mileage will be reduced by the qualifying amount for that award. You then will have 12 new months to accumulate more mileage and awards.

Travel awards are non-taxable and may be issued in your name or the name of any individual you designate. Once issued, they are non-transferable.

American offers you many mileage bonus opportunities.

For instance, *whenever* you fly First Class on American, you will receive a 25% extra mileage bonus in addition to your trip mileage.

But that's just for starters. New bonuses are continually in store for you—Double Mileage flights, Automatic Bonus Miles, and more!

You will be surprised at how quickly your mileage accumulates with all these bonuses coming your way on American. And it's all so easy!

American's computer tracking system works to your AAdvantage.

Our unique computer tracking system keeps you up to date on your AAdvantage progress by automatically recording all your trips. We will send you a Mileage Summary statement monthly, detailing each of your flights on American, accrued mileage per flight*, and any bonus miles credited as well as your total accumulated mileage. So all you have to do is fly. American does the rest.

*Mileage will be credited on the basis of CAB-approved nonstop distances between the cities where your flight originates and terminates. On connecting flights, you will receive mileage credit for each segment of your trip. on thru flights, you will receive the nonstop origin-destination mileage.

AmericanAirlines A'Advantage Application

Mr   Ms.
Mrs: Miss

_____ _____ _____
(First)   (Middle Initial)   (Last)

(Home Address)

_____ _____
                                    (Zip)

If you normally book through a Travel Agency. please indicate agency name

AmericanAirlines

EARN 2 FREE FIRST CLASS ROUND-TRIP TICKETS TO ANYWHERE WE FLY!

A'Advantage |
AmericanAirlines

A'Advantage℠ Application

talk to its best customers. Developed and quickly copied in 1981, the AAdvantage program simply awarded miles into a mileage account for every flight flown. These miles could then be used for free flights or trip upgrades. (See Exhibit 4.7.)

Perhaps the most fascinating part of watching the frequent flyer programs over the years has been their constant change. Once the AAdvantage program was in place, American had an ongoing communication vehicle to talk to and reward its best customers. As business travelers' mileage levels increased, they were rewarded with even higher levels of mileage points, 25% and 50% bonuses every time they flew. Flying the competition, no matter what the price or schedule, simply was not worth *not* getting your AAdvantage points. American had locked out the competition in the very competitive skies of business travel.

These frequent flyer programs began to be viewed as strategic tools. We saw a year of triple mileage for most clubs as one airline led the way to build their flyer base. We frequently saw offers of double and triple miles for customers who sampled new flight services or used different hub connections. Hotels and car rental companies quickly joined the programs to get in on the loyalty.

The latest round of awards comes via an upscale catalog of discounts and refunds AAdvantage members can receive in exchange for their miles. Like free flights, these awards are very targeted, with luxury items selected to appeal to business travelers—furs, vacation homes, sailboats, and fine jewelry. And the upgrades and offerings will continue as the nation's largest airlines fight to control the flight habits of the valuable business traveler.

AT&T Opportunity Calling

As the airlines were revelling in the opportunity to talk directly to their best customers and offer them something for their continued loyalty, another deregulated industry chose to follow the same database path. AT&T launched "Opportunity Calling" in 1984 as a way to add value and build loyalty with their consumer and business base of users. While other telephone companies were offering samples of their product in free telephone calls and waived switching charges, AT&T legally was barred from using its own product as an incentive. So the company turned to manufacturers of other products and services to offer billions of dollars in rebates. AT&T customers accumulated a point for every dollar of their long distance telephone bill. These points were used on goods and services offered in quarterly catalogs.

Holding the world's largest database of customers and their telephone usage patterns, AT&T took to research and customized versions of opportunity callers' catalogs, delivering targeted offers to homes sorted by lifestyle PRIZM codes. Urban customers received special offers at local businesses and restaurants where they could use their accumulated points. And even charities could benefit, with donation drives for Special Olympics being used to help clear out some of the liability of unused points in the universe of Opportunity Calling homes.

Where the airline industry and others were successful in offering truly compelling awards, AT&T was barred from offering what people really wanted from their long distance service—better prices. As AT&T matured as a marketing force in a competitive environment and was able to price its services competitively, the need for the borrowed interest and awards from Opportunity Calling waned. Programs that more directly address customers' usage like Reach Out America pricing packages, Calling Cards and now credit cards that offer long distance savings have replaced the massive added-value stopgap promotion AT&T used during the highly competitive deregulation days. (See Exhibit 4.8.)

Maxwell House Coffee

While special events and sponsorship burst into marketing plans in the '80s, very few marketers took the extra step to make their event involvement really pay off at retail. Maxwell House went

EXHIBIT 4.8

event involvement really pay off at retail. Maxwell House went beyond the objectives of exposure and building positive brand image by linking retail promotions with Taste of Chicago, the multimillion-people event at Chicago's lakefront over Independence Day.

Using a simple incentive of giving $6.00 in free Taste of Chicago food tickets in exchange for empty Maxwell House coffee cans, the company took the market by storm. Customized POS at retail called attention to the offer as did newspaper ads. A sampling and redemption booth at the event sent crowds back to the stores to buy more coffee for more valuable free tickets for the two-week event.

As other brand sponsors got lost in the multitude of sponsors at the event, Maxwell House brought the promotion home to where sales made all the difference . . . retail.

McDonald's Monopoly

What do you get when you team two American institutions together for a collect and win game? Super sales and a very fun event. McDonald's borrowed the universal appeal of the classic Parker Bros. board game of Monopoly as the theme and collection device for a traffic-building game in 1987. It had been a few years since a big, memorable game had been used, so America was ready for it. The prizes and mechanics were fairly basic. What was great was the simplicity and sheer fun of playing, reinforcing McDonald's basic premise of good food and fun. For everyone who ever tried for Boardwalk and Park Place, this game was a success. (See Exhibit 4.9.)

Macintosh Computers

Out of all the promotions of the '80s, "Test Drive a Macintosh" typifies the very best in strategy and execution. Here was Apple's most sophisticated, yet user-friendly model. Though expensive, users found that once they started with it, the Mac

EXHIBIT 4.9

people's homes and offices to let them see first-hand how wonderful this computer could be.

Creatively, Apple looked to a concept we all know—the test drive. The company invited consumers to take a Mac home and try it. And this sampling program worked. After a simple trial run, most test drivers were sold and bought the Macintosh. This classically simple promotion was delivered with style and excitement, just like the computer. (See Exhibit 4.10.)

The Sweet Smell of Vanderbilt Success

Just as packaged goods promotion flourished in the '70s because of inflation and generics, the '80s saw real growth for the sales promotion industry with new industries and categories entering the arena. Services and transportation companies became major promoters. And everyone began to borrow promotion successes from packaged goods marketers.

Channels of distribution that had never supported promotions before were opened up to capture the consumers' attention. Upscale department stores, boutiques, and specialty stores recognized that their customers were the same people participating in promotions at the supermarket or buying lottery tickets at the drugstore.

This review of a very successful program shows one of the first promotions to be accepted and very successful at the department store fragrance counter. You'll see how effective a traditional package goods promotion can be when image and prestige are brought to the forefront.

The Vanderbilt Situation

It was Year 2 of the most successful new fragrance introduction in America's history. How can you maintain that excitement and record sales after such success? How do you keep retailers'

EXHIBIT 4.10

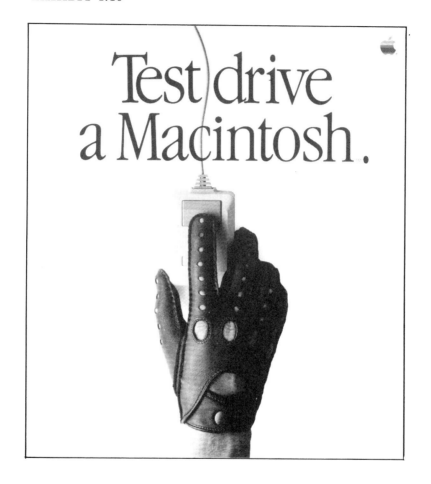

attention in two very disparate distribution channels—upscale department stores with their fickleness toward fashion, and drug and mass merchandisers where other new products fight to replace anything not performing at maximum levels?

The situation called for "smoke and excitement" to carry on the imagery and enchantment begun the previous year. And it had to speak to the retailer and staff to push and display the brand as well as to the consumer to pull the product out at retail.

Objectives

1. Gain consumer trial as a first step towards increased sales.
2. Continue building awareness of the brand, especially at distribution outlets.
3. Extend the luxurious, upscale image of the brand.

Strategies

1. Use a sweepstakes to carry on the brand excitement from the initial successful launch and to continue to build awareness.
2. Use truly elegant prizes to extend the image and capture the attention and imagination of the target audience.
3. Sample all entrants by including a scent strip on the entry form as well as mailing an actual sample bottle of perfume to all who enter.
4. Offer store clerks the chance to win wonderful prizes.
5. Force customers to the retail display to pick up an entry, therefore driving traffic to retail.
6. Support the promotion with substantial advertising and high quality trade and display materials.

The Winning Big Idea

Beautiful creative execution and prizes drove this promotion's success. The "Flight of Fantasy" sweepstakes (using the Vanderbilt fragrance advertising theme) captured women's imaginations at all levels. From Bloomingdale's and Marshall Field's to J.C. Penney and Walgreen's, store clerks were eligible to win

EXHIBIT 4.11

EXHIBIT 4.12

cultured pearls or leather luggage, just for mailing an entry card found in displays. Or they could win gifts from Cartier Jewelers, sterling dinnerware or dining-out certificates if one of their customers won a prize.

The splendor of Vanderbilt appealed to women everywhere with a Grand Prize of a true "Vanderbilt" vacation with the Concorde, the Orient Express, and limousines in every European city. This very rich sweepstakes recognized everyone who entered, with a 2 ml bottle of Vanderbilt perfume mailed to each entrant's home. Even the entry form carried a scent strip for sampling and four pages of romance copy that continued to build the image of elegance.

The Results

Warner Cosmetics, the sponsoring company, reported a resounding success. Year 2 sales surpassed expectations in all distribution channels, proving that upscale, image-conscious department and specialty stores will support the right promotions. And sell-thru at retail was exceptionally strong as women zeroed in on displays to receive entry forms.

Sometimes, real promotion breakthroughs come from standard, tried and true techniques. It's taking these known successes and introducing them into new industries or distribution channels that can make a magnificent impact.

Owning Your Own Sales Promotion Business

The one thing you learn in your own business is that you never stop learning. So I've pulled together some of the things I've learned over the past 30 years while running my agency in the hopes that my lessons may offer insight or inspiration to any readers owning or contemplating starting up their own businesses.

1. Planning for your own business requires emotional, physical and financial savings. You start saving up your energy. You save up or borrow money. And most importantly, you save and grow your courage.
2. Constantly analyze your situation. Take a look at the marketplace. Look at your personnel. Structure your company around the business you have, the people you have and the opportunities that present themselves. And don't be afraid to change if you feel you can make an improvement.
3. Be obsessive about making your customers happy. Without them you don't have a business.
4. If you're not a risktaker, if you're not willing to be scared, don't go into business for yourself. No matter how well you plan, there will be surprises. And it seems the larger the business gets, the bigger the surprises get.
5. In your own business, you sell and you yell. All the time. And the successful business owners will be those who know and consistently balance these two activities.
6. Be prepared to work 12 hours a day, 7 days a week. There is little time for reading for pleasure or watching a movie to relax because you should always have a part of you keeping an eye out for an idea or thought for your clients.
7. Have enough money for 18-24 months of bad business. That's payroll, rent, utilities, insurance payments, everything your company is responsible for paying.
8. Dare to be different.

Selling Your Own Sales Promotion Business

If you do all the above things right, at some point you'll need to address this topic—selling your business. Once again, I'll share some insights.

1. Don't take it too personally. This can be one of the most gut-wrenching steps in your lifetime. You are not just

opening your books and your business to potential buyers, but you're exposing your style, your business acumen and every success and failure you've met along the way. Potential buyers are not judging you nearly as much as they are judging your business.

2. Take it very personally. You know your company and it's environment and people's strengths and philosophies better than any one else. Try to find a buyer that will make a good fit. Especially pay attention to this point if you're staying on for awhile.

3. Learn all you can about the process. It's fascinating to see how financial people can assign values to the intangibles you've collected. Talk to other sellers in other industries for creative financing and acceptable negotiating points. Be smart about the business.

4. Make it happen. Selling a business often means making a big lifestyle change. And those changes are very easy to put off. But don't procrastinate the process and the decisions. You need to put as much effort into making it happen as you do building new business or any other business plan.

5. Live with your decision. There will be tough times when you're no longer the boss and your fine judgment is overruled. You'll probably have different priorities than the new owners. And they'll want to make changes. And they can. Yet you can also graciously help guide their way and you'll all come out better in the long run.

Lessons from the Eighties

While it's still early to predict what advances from the '80s made the strongest impact on marketing, we're confident that these trends will live on:

- Frequent flyer/loyalty programs are now an important part of marketing, especially with targeted products.

- Technology at store level will open more promotion doors. Scanners at supermarket cash registers gave retailers the upper hand on product movement that led to slotting allowances, new product failure fees, and an even heavier hand dealing with manufacturers. The pluses of scanners include better product movement data, faster and less expensive supermarket checker operations and some very interesting promotion opportunities—electronic continuity programs and competitive couponing, for example.

- Clutter continues as an even bigger issue than ever before. The number of weekly commercials on network television alone has risen from about 2,500 in 1971 to over 6,100 in 1990. We'll keep seeing interesting attempts at catching our attention—from holograms delivered in magazines to talking point of sale displays and promotional television.

CHAPTER FIVE

The Future of Promotional Marketing—A Whole New Ballgame

Futurists and historians claim that the final decade in a century sees incredible progress as world inhabitants try to make up for transgressions committed during the previous 90 years. There's an unconscious drive of human nature that views the turn of the century as a deadline for problems and programs that need completion.

Early in the final decade we witnessed "kinder and gentler" actions throughout the world. Then we swiftly moved to war in the Middle East. Starting with the fall of the Berlin Wall through a universal cry for saving the Earth's ecology, we saw changes that offered a new world—and new opportunities for marketing and promotion.

A generation grew up without an international war but with domestic urban problems like drugs, gangs, and the homeless. (See Exhibit 5.1.) The 1991 war in the Gulf suddenly thrust young people into combat and war into our homes through CNN news. We have almost outgrown our mass media technology as computers allow personalization and more speed for information than ever before.

So we're looking at some interesting times ahead. Let's see where marketing and promotion will fit in the future.

The Greening of Supermarket Shelves

It didn't take long for marketers to catch on to the news value of and the consumer preference for ecologically-improved products and packaging. And opportunities will continue to position and promote new or restaged products that don't harm the Earth. "Green" products, like truly recyclable diapers and minimally packaged detergents, are in their infancy.

We're seeing products positioned and marketed purely on their Earth-friendly benefits. Ben & Jerry's Ice Cream is made with ingredients chosen to supplement the economies of Rain Forest territories. Dow Chemical has taken to the high schools to start early education on the benefits of recycling. McDonald's has pledged to turn around its bad-guy image with plastics and overpackaging and to convert to recycled papers.

Retailers are giving preference to "green" products, some flagging environmentally friendly products with special point of sale in stores, others authorizing only safe products for introduction. Just as we saw the "no cholesterol" and "hearthealthy" bandwagon in the '80s, we can expect comparable hoopla with new packaging and bold claims in the future. Expect to see promotional tie-ins with environment groups, especially at the grass roots level, and plenty of thematic promotions with "green themes."

EXHIBIT 5.1 "Kinder and gentler" promotions reflect the tone of America. Look for more cause marketing efforts from category leaders like Crest as they hold loyalty without talking price. Reprinted with permission.

International Barriers Fall

A whole new world for marketing is opening as the walls of communism tumble and people throughout the world clamor for American products and choices. Comparable to America in the '50s, we're facing economies in countries with a pent-up demand for our products and marketing. The opening of the Single Market in Western Europe is another opportunity for global products and messages.

In the world of advertising, U.S. agencies have been planning on "going international" for years, with research on global communications and mergers or affiliations with local advertising agencies in most civilized countries. Marketing services agencies have not been as aggressive in international planning, and with good reason. The retail situation and products and services in general just aren't ready for promotion. No one needs to be forced to sample products or buy services. The new economies are anxious to try Western goods and sample the American lifesyle. Aggressive promotion will come later.

What promotion agencies should be doing now, however, is planning for the near future when competition heats up and promotion becomes an issue. Agencies should be forming affiliations with potential partners throughout the world. And all of us in promotional marketing should become familiar with the marketing cultures of the countries into which current clients may be expanding or building distribution channels.

In time, there will be a whole world of opportunities for forward-thinking marketers who "go global."

Smaller Worlds for the Nineties

As new markets open throughout the world, some of America's markets are getting much smaller. Niche marketing, the creation and positioning of limited, targeted products, continues to grow.

Computers and technology have allowed us to pinpoint very specific audiences for some products and quickly assess their profit potential. Targeted direct mail, in-store communications, and narrow casting as in cable broadcasting, can zero in on those people most likely to need or buy these fine-tuned products.

Image building is key in niche markets, as well as sampling and trial. So we see private liqueur tastings and car or computer test drives with image-enhancing incentives to try. We've seen an entire industry of loyalty-building, frequent-flyer type programs, designed to talk only to current customers, encouraging them to stay brand-exclusive and heavily rewarding those customers that do.

Starting off the '90s are many promotions aimed directly at children. Packaged goods marketers like Kool-Aid and Kraft Macaroni & Cheese have recognized the importance of kids' preference now and for the future and are rewarding kids and moms for ongoing support. (See Exhibit 5.2.)

Ethnic promotions will extend beyond Black and Hispanic groups to Asian Americans, Indians, and Middle East immigrants. Each of these targets represents profitable marketing opportunities as the ethnic communities look for acceptance and "home country" products here.

New, More Powerful Media

Niche marketing appears to be a wave for the future. Smaller-reach, more targeted and responsive media will bring us closer to direct consumers. Marketers are turning away from mass media vehicles like network television and large daily newspapers in favor of specialized media, such as targeted direct mail and videotext. Kids are growing up with not just television, but video games, VCR video rentals, and targeted cable as a way of life. Reading is, unfortunately, becoming less and less popular with kids, forcing newspapers to rethink their standard fare and promote to elementary and high schools to try to hang on to readers for another generation.

EXHIBIT 5.2 Building brand loyalty will be a critical issue for the '90s. Kraft leads the way by starting kids off with their own Cheese & Macaroni Club that rewards frequent usage with targeted fun prizes. Reprinted with permission.

In-store, instant-gratification vehicles match the faster-pace of the media and cause more impulse decisions. Store videocarts and talking store displays will capture those consumers who now skip newspapers and other promotional media for coupons and offers. Retailers, having rejected store point of sale shelf clutter, will lead the way, with customer reward programs, driven by scanner technology, taking creative promotions even further from the shelves.

The Search for Alternatives to Discounts

The quest for added-value promotions will become even more important as marketers in all categories recognize the downward profit spiral that unchecked price promoting can bring to their categories. We have seen the auto rebates of the '70s and '80s totally undermine the real price/value relationship in car sales. We've seen packaged goods categories fight for survival amid on-pack coupon wars and heavy trade discounting. The airlines continue with their fare reductions that fill seats but force up the cost of full-fare business passengers.

In an effort to keep brands from becoming commodities selected purely on price, marketers are looking to add value and possibly build loyalty with each purchase. Frequent-buyer programs are just one approach that most marketers have, at least, considered. Others are tie-in promotions that no longer just reduce the price of the promoted brand, but offer related items at savings or free.

Some of the biggest changes we're seeing are at the retail level. In the hopes of getting out from under heavy trade allowances, manufacturers are going to the trade with programs that build business, not just the bottom line. Hence we've seen the rise of promotional menus and customized promotions that allow retailers to run promotions that work to the store's objectives, not just the brand's. Manufacturers that offer DPP-based planagrams, space-saving packaging, customized pallet programs,

EXHIBIT 5.3 Customized promotions like this Osco Sweepstakes will continue as long as retailer's objectives are met. Reprinted with permission of Osco Drug.

or labor-saving store-to-door delivery are helping build business and the relationship with the retailer. (See Exhibit 5.3.)

Deca-Trends—The Marketing Challenge of the Nineties

As we've looked back at the last 40 years we've seen the distance promotion has come. From starting as simple displays and sales aids to database marketing and guerilla coupon delivery, promotion has risen in corporate ranks as *the* way to impact sales now and in the future. So what does that leave for the future? What's the challenge?

Managing promotional marketing is the issue for the forward thinking company. Promotion can no longer be defined in the 1980s terms as "a short-term inducement to increase sales." It has taken on a new definition. Promotional marketing is both short- and long-term sales inducements which are consistently image- and franchise-building.

The Age of Marketing Surplus

Looking at the dynamics of the promotion marketplace, we see promotion spending growing at about 14 percent annually since the early '80s. At this rate, we'll see a doubling of promotion spending in the early '90s. That means twice the coupons. Twice the frequent-user programs. Twice the rebates, the Super Saver fares, the new car financing plans.

All this promotional activity will be focused on a consumer population that is at close to zero-base growth. We can anticipate twice the offers for close to twice the products and media aimed at the same size consumer base as we see today.

And that adds up to a decline in promotion effectiveness. We're beginning to see this already, with significant declines in coupon redemption rates as the first indication of promotion overload. As we saw in Chapter 4, redemption rates have declined from an average of 3.9 percent in 1983 to 3.2 percent in 1988. In a five-year period coupon redemption declined almost 20 percent in effectiveness.

As any marketer knows, it is becoming increasingly difficult to be noticed amid the clutter. We have a *marketing surplus*—more products, more promotions, more distribution points, and more media vehicles than ever before.

A New Format for Success

Saturation is forcing marketers and their promotion partners to face new issues. Not only is it mandatory for promotions to meet the traditional goal—achieve short-term sales results—but now we must meet these new goals. Smart marketers are challenging their promotions to:

- **Meet quantifiable objectives**. Now, more than ever before, marketers are devoting the time and energies in quantifying their promotion expectations and results. What had been lip service to research is now a legitimate challenge.
- **Deliver strategic programming**. Just a promotion no longer works. Now we need promotion events that strategically combine promotional advertising, publicity, and offers that build brand image, not just sell products.
- **Zero in on precise targets**. As products are becoming more niche-oriented, so should promotions. Make the messages and the offers more compelling by talking directly to the best targets.
- **Focus on the distribution points**. Expand distribution or drive traffic by including the distribution element in the planning stages. This may be as simple as co-op advertising for the promotion or as complex as using related retailers or products to promote your promotion.
- **Create intrusive programs**. Execution can no longer just

be good. First and foremost, promotions *must* get attention. This can mean creative use of media, creative offers, or creative artwork. Whatever gets attention.

- **Deliver purchases and image enhancement.** As more traditional advertising dollars are being channeled into promotional advertising, more responsibility to build the brand is being placed on promotions. This could mean fewer borrowed-interest promotions in the future and more events that sell image and product benefits.

Techniques for the Nineties

1. New Technology

The computer age continues to bring new opportunities for marketing. Some of the most interesting advances are in the stores: shopping cart-activated video developed by ActMedia that plays commercials as shoppers near displays, and frequent shopper database programs developed by Citibank that record shoppers' purchases as they are happening. Other technical wonders are sweepstakes and sampling programs for computer programs delivered on actual disks mailed or inserted in magazines to computer users. The key for the '90s is assume that technology can do whatever you need to be done. Someone, somewhere will have the answer.

2. Continuity Plus

If the '80s was the age of the frequent-flyer program, the '90s takes that trend one step further. American Airlines' AAdvantage Program now offers upscale watches, furs, and summer homes for the travelers who want an alternative to getting on another plane. The next step in continuity can take many forms, all playing directly to the heavy user and offering some form of lock-in device. For example, American Express Buyers' Assurance Program was the first to unconditionally guarantee anything bought with the card. Even Kool-Aid's wacky warehouse locks Mom into buying Kool Aid because of the wild and wacky free gifts with proofs of purchase. (See Exhibit 5.4.)

3. *Targeted Promotions*

Hand in hand with technological advances will come almost unlimited opportunities for marketers to talk directly to their best customers. Targeting can be geographical, with local programs that bring promotions to the target. J&B Scotch did this with gift wrapping vans in Manhattan during the busy holiday shopping time. Other targeted efforts aim at decision makers—Federal Express, for example, introduced *networking*, a newsletter aimed at the needs and interests of secretaries and professional support staff. Targeting will continue as we solicit our current customers and heavy users to begin dialogues with these important markets. (See Exhibit 5.5.)

4. *Special Events*

While events rose to popularity in the '80s, the '90s will demand more brand action for the sponsorship dollar. Especially now that packaged goods manufacturers are jumping on the race car and sports circuits, promotions will need to close the loop of sponsorship at retail. Expect to see more event-related premiums at POS, some discounts on admission with proofs of purchase or involvement activities at retail. Events that offer sampling opportunities will need to carry more bounceback purchase incentives to convert these triers to users.

5. *New Media Use*

In the '60s the advertising community lamented the increase in commercial clutter on television. Today we're overwhelmed with multiple FSIs and jammed mail boxes. To capture attention in this busy world, smart marketers will be looking for new ways to use the media. Hallmark cards continues to sample their Shoebox Greeting cards by inserting an actual card or envelope in targeted publications. Perfume samples in magazines are run-of-the-mill. But L'Oreal caught the eye of plenty of young women when it ran actual eye shadow samples in magazines. And Christmas

EXHIBIT 5.4 Wacky Warehouse gifts will keep Moms buying Kool-Aid for their kids to accumulate points for free gifts and club activities like free bowling. Reprinted with permission.

EXHIBIT 5.5 Federal Express recognized the importance of secretaries in the purchase decision and developed the "Networking" newsletter to this niche. Reprinted with permission.

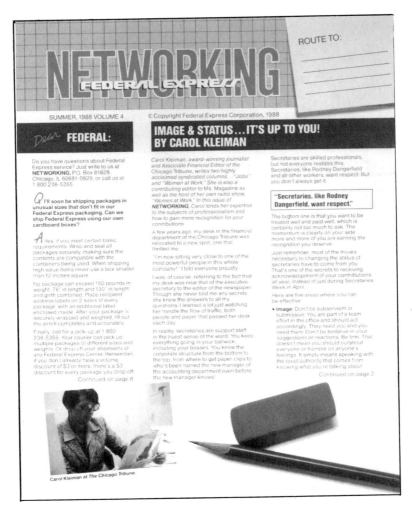

NETWORKING
FEDERAL EXPRESS

ROUTE TO:

SUMMER, 1988 VOLUME 4   © Copyright Federal Express Corporation, 1988

Dear FEDERAL:

Do you have questions about Federal Express service? Just write to us at **NETWORKING**, P.O. Box 81829, Chicago, IL 60681-0829, or call us at 1 800 238-5355.

Q I'll soon be shipping packages in unusual sizes that don't fit in our Federal Express packaging. Can we ship Federal Express using our own cardboard boxes?

A Yes, if you meet certain basic requirements. Wrap and seal all packages securely, making sure the contents are compatible with the containers being used. When shipping high value items never use a box smaller than 12 inches square.

No package can exceed 150 pounds in weight, 76" in length and 130" in length and girth combined. Place recipient address labels on 2 sides of every package with an additional label enclosed inside. After your package is securely wrapped and weighed, fill out the airbill completely and accurately.

Finally, call for a pick-up at 1 800 238-5355. Your courier can pick up multiple packages of different sizes and weights. Or drop off your shipments at any Federal Express Center. Remember, if you don't already have a volume discount of $3 or more, there's a $3 discount for every package you drop off.

Continued on page 8

IMAGE & STATUS... IT'S UP TO YOU!
BY CAROL KLEIMAN

Carol Kleiman, award-winning journalist and Associate Financial Editor of the Chicago Tribune, writes two highly acclaimed syndicated columns... "Jobs" and "Women at Work." She is also a contributing editor to Ms. Magazine as well as the host of her own radio show, "Women at Work." In this issue of NETWORKING, Carol lends her expertise to the subjects of professionalism and how to gain more recognition for your contributions.

A few years ago, my desk in the financial department of the Chicago Tribune was relocated to a new spot, one that thrilled me.

"I'm now sitting very close to one of the most powerful people in this whole company!" I told everyone proudly.

I was, of course, referring to the fact that my desk was near that of the executive secretary to the editor of the newspaper. Though she never told me any secrets, she knew the answers to all my questions. I learned a lot just watching her handle the flow of traffic, both people and paper that passed her desk each day.

In reality, secretaries are support staff in the truest sense of the word. You keep everything going in your bailiwick, including your bosses. You know the corporate structure from the bottom to the top, from where to get paper clips to who's been named the new manager of the accounting department even before the new manager knows!

Secretaries are skilled professionals, but not everyone realizes this. Secretaries, like Rodney Dangerfield and all other workers, want respect. But you don't always get it.

> **"Secretaries, like Rodney Dangerfield, want respect."**

The bottom line is that you want to be treated well and paid well, which is certainly not too much to ask. The momentum is clearly on your side ... more and more of you are earning the recognition you deserve.

Just remember, most of the moves necessary to changing the status of secretaries have to come from you. That's one of the secrets to receiving acknowledgement of your contributions all year, instead of just during Secretaries Week in April.

Here are five areas where you can be effective.

• **Image**: Don't be subservient or submissive. You are part of a team effort in the office and should act accordingly. They need you and you need them. Don't be tentative in your suggestions or reactions. Be firm. That doesn't mean you should outshout everyone or trample on anyone's feelings. It simply means speaking with the quiet authority that comes from knowing what you're talking about.

Continued on page 2

Carol Kleiman at *The Chicago Tribune.*

has become a media event as we look forward to the liquor companies trying to outdo Absolut with unique magazine treatments. All for impact. (See Exhibit 5.6.)

6. *Trade Leveraging*

Marketers are finding that retailers can be powerful friends when it comes to promotion. Rather than coast with straight co-op advertising or allowances, Kodak has been teaming with retailers to offer partner programs that bring significantly stronger results to both partners. Some retailers get traffic building sweepstakes for which customers must enter at the camera department. Other retailers have customized film packaging that offers photoprocessing specials back at the retailers. In turn, retailers are accepting, displaying, and featuring the growing array of Kodak products. And everyone wins.

7. *Marketing Synergy*

Have you noticed more promotion *events*? More activities like Bud Bowl I, II, and III that tie in events, television, magazine ads, and point of sale materials? Marketers are looking beyond traditional promotion avenues and are incorporating as many visibility and involvement outlets as possible. CBS and NBC both took retail partners to help capture viewers for their new seasons with K-Mart and Sears. And the participating retailers shared in the excitement with added traffic. Orville Redenbacher popcorn stands out at video stores as an impulse purchase and add-on sales for the video retailer. More and more marketers are looking for promotion agencies with capabilities in broadcast or connections in Hollywood to make their promotions go a little further. (See Exhibit 5.7.)

8. *Consumer Involvement*

This is a personal favorite, a challenge I make to our folks with every promotion recommendation. How can we get the consumer more involved? Because once they're involved

EXHIBIT 5.6 Smart marketers are continuing to search for new ways to utilize the media. Hallmark has had success with sampling their Shoebox Greetings cards in targeted publications. Reprinted with permission.

At Hallmark, we've always given away free envelopes with our cards. Well, guess what...

Now we're giving away free cards with our envelopes.

SHOEBOX GREETINGS
(A tiny little division of Hallmark)

EXHIBIT 5.7 Retailers heading into the 1990s have joined forces with the networks to increase their promotional options. CBS and NBC turned to K-Mart and Sears for promotional partnerships. Reprinted with permission.

EXHIBIT 5.8 Kool-Aid courts Mom with real involvement in a "Do-It-Yourself" coupon ad that lets her choose her incentive. Reprinted with permission.

EXHIBIT 5.9 Holiday liquor advertising reaches far for reader involvement. Here Crown Royal asks readers to create their own ad with stickers and a blank format. Reprinted with permission.

they've made a commitment to the promotion and the brand. Expect more telemarketing 800- and 900-number promotions or more "do-it-yourself" ads. One great example that caught readers' attention was a Kool-Aid FSI ad that invited readers to select a free product to get when they bought Kool-Aid. The catch came as readers were instructed to cut out the free product visual and attach it to the Kool-Aid coupon for validation. This execution got involvement while offering a significant value. (See Exhibit 5.8.) Seagrams Crown Royal gave readers a chance to build their own ad with an adult version of kids' stickers. It was hard for even the stuffiest fine whiskey drinker to pass up the holiday magazine premium. (See Exhibit 5.9.)

Other simpler involvement devices to use are contests (remember the '50s?) and the favorite "scratch 'n sniff" and "rub 'n reveal" print techniques. Anything that gets the targeted consumers' attention!

These trends give some direction for the future. We believe that if you keep one eye on how trends like these can benefit your brand and one eye on where your brand needs to be in the future, you'll be heading into the next century in the lead.

Creative Flares Fire Up and Fade

We've seen those creative trends in advertising where one breakthrough idea wins awards and everyone else follows suit. Did anyone *not* get tired of hearing old '60s music resurrected to sell products in the '80s? And after Pepsi bought Michael Jackson, then Coke bought George Michaels and Madonna, and Pepsi bought Michael J. Fox or was that Diet Pepsi? Or Diet Coke? Or Diet Dr. Pepper? And who cares?

We've had some of our own interesting creative trends in sales promotion over the years. Some have been driven by technology—no one wants to be the first to try it, but everyone wants to be the second.

Early-on promotions, like most advertising of the booming '50s, were tremendously copy-heavy. Reading, especially magazines, was still the way the world was brought into homes in the pre-TV days. So promotions entertained while offering contest prizes and product promises primarily through the printed word. Even pictures were mostly illustrated to make prizes and products look bigger (and better) than real life. (See Exhibit 5.10)

Television forced some real changes in creative execution. First, it made America much more graphic-oriented than copy-oriented. Pictures became worth more than 1,000 words when we demanded to see rather than hear or read about promotions. This marked the end of long copy ads and promotions so that, today, the only long copy you see in promotions has been written by lawyers for contest rules and conditions of entry.

Second, truth in advertising and the consumer movement, coupled with photography, film, and printing advances made photography a better alternative to illustration. As Campbell's Soup was no longer able to "augment" the meat and vegetables in their soup photography by using a base of marbles in the bowl, promoters in general were no longer allowed to illustrate or show their product or prizes in an unrealistic, exaggerated way. Additionally, testimonial advertising came under scrutiny and so we saw doctors and actors no longer "recommending" products but major new "spokescritters" on the scene. The Pillsbury Doughboy, Tony the Tiger for Frosted Flakes, Charlie Tuna for Star*Kist; the Jolly Green Giant and Morris the Cat for 9 Lives—all were born from the creative stables at Leo Burnett. The Frito Bandito was introduced to represent the crunchy corn taste of Fritos Corn Chips; Sinclair gas had Dino the Dinosaur; Enco gas had tigers in our tanks; the symbols were starting strong. And we hadn't even been introduced to the red-haired clown from McDonald's yet! These very creative spokescharacters worked well to make a memorable impression on consumers.

EXHIBIT 5.10 Creative execution in the '50s was mostly copy-oriented like this brand-building contest for Ford. Then marketers learned that a picture is worth a thousand words. Reprinted with permission.

And they offered outstanding promotion opportunities that are still being used today.

Using celebrities and events as borrowed interest to attract attention continues. The '70s brought an interesting refund ploy using celebrities that actually had consumers *not* cashing their checks. Very simply, refund checks were "signed" by a celebrity. In the innocent '70s there were still people who believed these were real and collected a Joe Namath or Hank Aaron signature. The really interesting collectible checks were those signed by our advertising "spokespeople" like Mr. Whipple and Morris the Cat.

"Involvement" became a buzzword in the late '70s as marketers tried harder for their promotions to stand out from others. One of the bandwagons that promotion creatives jumped on was the match and win sweepstakes. As a novelty, packaged goods manufacturers were almost guaranteed of getting a display up in grocery stores, if customers would be coming in with game pieces to see if they won a prize. But what retailers once perceived to be a real traffic-generating activity soon went sour. The "trend" quickly became an overused tactic which no longer got retail display support. Smart marketers quickly switched customers from matching game pieces to displays to matching them to the actual product—either a logo or UPC—expecting customers to put the product in their shopping carts rather than back on the shelf after comparing game pieces. (See Exhibit 5.14.)

Instant win sweepstakes took over after match and win. Cracker Jack was the first to overcome legal restrictions and the "no purchase necessary" rule to offer a real surprise in each box. Along with the small toy that America expected to find, was a game piece that might award a real car—not just a toy car. By offering free game pieces by mail, marketers could get around the long-time lottery rules that state manufacturers cannot require purchase while delivering the ultimate excitement with instant win. Now shoppers weren't just getting a can of tomatoes or a pair of panty hose. Now they were getting a chance for a bundle of gold or $10,000.

Still a popular approach, we've seen some wonderful creative

EXHIBIT 5.11 Oscar Mayer hot dogs looked back to its 1950–60s images to bring back a Wiener Whistle premium in 1990. Reprinted courtesy of Oscar Mayer Foods Corporation. Oscar Mayer and the Oscar Mayer rhomboid are registered trademarks of Oscar Mayer Foods Corporation.

EXHIBIT 5.12 Clever use of celebrities, including "autographs" on refund checks, helped build interest and glamor in promotions. This 1972 Mennon event shared the popularity of World Heavyweight Champ, Joe Frazier. Reprinted with permission.

EXHIBIT 5.13 Kid appeal comes from the borrowed interest of the World Wrestling Federation in this promotion for Planters Lifesavers candies. Reprinted with permission.

EXHIBIT 5.14 After "match-and-win sweepstakes" displays peaked in popularity, manufacturers sent consumers to the product to match game pieces. Fast retail turns for Fritos® brand Corn Chips made it easy to offer "match and win" right on the package. Reprinted with permission.

executions from this tactic. Ralston cereals gave away toy Corvettes in its cereals—and if you were lucky enough to get a red one, you'd also get a real red Corvette! Playing off Ivory's unique feature of being the brand that floats, the soap offered $10,000 to the holder of Ivory soap bars that sunk.

The biggest instant win promotion that had record-breaking potential was Coke's 1990 MagiCan promotion that had money popping from one of every 20 cans. A few technical rejects and heavy consumer backlash caused the promotion to end early, with a major Coke recall in the heaviest usage season. While Coke's magic didn't last, there will be plenty more creative instant win games that capture sales and fun in the future.

It was American Express and the Statue of Liberty that started a landslide of cause-related promotions in the '80s that still continues. As President Reagan scaled back funding support for many public programs and institutions, corporate America was challenged with picking up the slack. And the marketing community found a perfect way to build brand preference by promoting products using charity overlays.

American Express found the ultimate charity to support—America—with the plan to save America's symbol of freedom to the world. Every time a cardholder made an American Express transaction, a small donation was made to a restoration fund to save the Statue of Liberty in time for her 100th birthday.

And the event became bigger as more corporate sponsors and major spokespeople became involved. Lee Iacocca and Chrysler made the Statue an American issue against Japanese cars. Stroh's Beer brought in other sponsors for the world's largest running race held in cities across America to benefit the Lady. (See Exhibit 5.15.)

Over $345 million dollars were raised for the Statue of Liberty and Ellis Island facelift with those corporate sponsors who promoted the loudest reaping the residual benefits the most. Borrowed interest in promotion was raised to an artform with the birth of cause marketing. Now brand choice and promotion participation depended more on the consumer's acceptance to own up to a cause instead of choosing a brand based on benefits

EXHIBIT 5.15 Stroh's headlined a major running race
fundraiser for the Statue of Liberty. Reprinted with permission.

or even image. Any brand, any product became more appealing, more important when sheathed in the cloak of freedom and the Statue of Liberty.

Following quickly on the success of the Statue of Liberty promotions were other gangbuster cause events. Live Aid brought together 162,000 concert goers at Kennedy Stadium in Philadelphia and at Wembly Stadium in London to hear rock musicians perform to raise funds for African Famine Relief. (See Exhibit 5.16.) An HBO all-day broadcast to over 1.5 billion viewers, caller donations, and major sponsors made the event an all-time biggest fundraiser. Over $100,000 million in public pledges were received. Even more importantly, it made charity ''cool'' to a whole new generation of children and young adults.

Package goods manufacturers quickly tied in with grassroots causes. Girl Scouts benefited from coupons redeemed for P&G soaps. Mothers Against Drunk Driving (MADD) sold coupons in retail-delivered books that benefited their cause. Dean's Milk led the cause to look for missing children by donating space on their cartons to show photographs of runaway or abducted children. Then, Trailways Bus Co. offered free bus transportation back home to the runaways.

Corporate America found they could benefit in plenty of ways from their generosity. Some companies chose to donate funds based on coupons redeemed, hoping to drive up redemption. Others chose to benefit from additional media and word-of-mouth exposure with public relations–based programs like the Trailways event. Some tied in with other companies for grand events such as Hands Across America that came close to forming a chain of people holding hands from coast-to-coast. Sponsors offered soft drink samples, T-shirts and displayed signage. And some simply chose to pay to attach their logo and provide trips for their customers to the grandest event held every four years— the Olympics.

These charity events were an easy way to borrow creative interest, especially for the new service marketers emerging into competitive areas for the first time—AT&T, airlines, Federal Express, IBM. Low interest products like paper products, clean-

EXHIBIT 5.16 Live Aid and all the participating musicians made charity ''cool'' to a whole new generation of young people. Reprinted with permission.

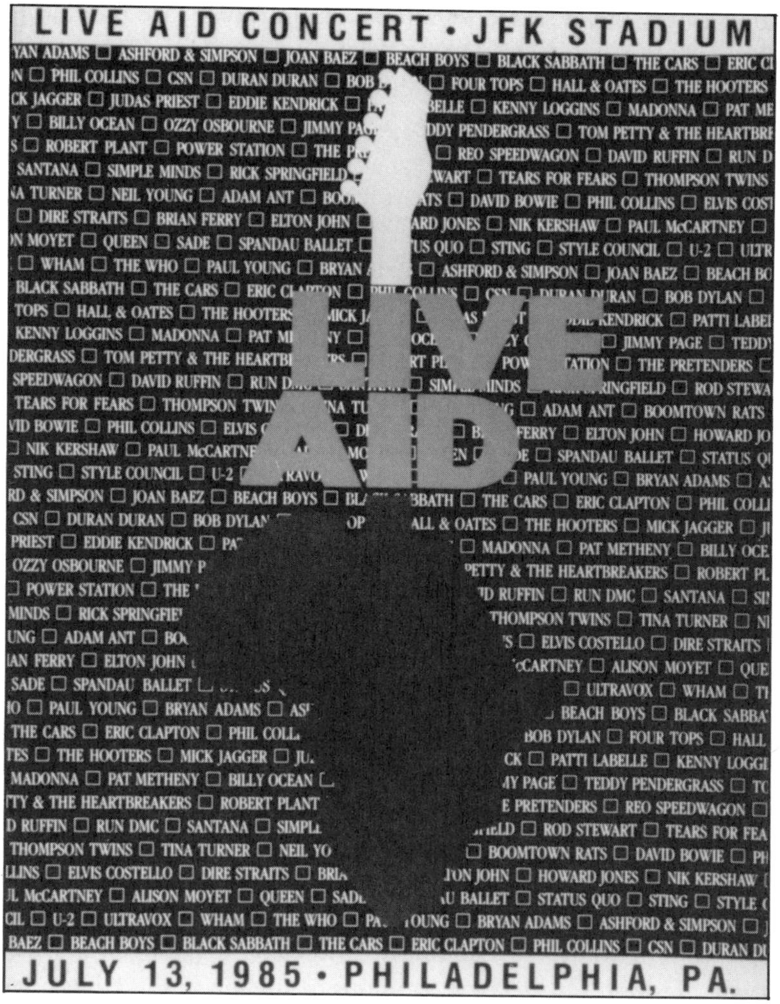

ers, health and beauty aids, and many food products found charity tie-ins to be a fast way to get attention, sales, and support from the trade. And the image-based brands—especially soft drinks, beer, and cigarettes—fought their way to lead the charge in event sponsorship.

But like any trend, we saw the build-up, the crest and the ebb happen—all within the '80s. The early '90s saw a return to more hard-hitting sales-driven promotions as if the collective boardrooms across corporate America said in unison "That was nice, now let's get back to business."

And as Wall Street and boardrooms have challenged companies to be more profitable, to cut costs, and to work harder, promotional marketing faces a similar challenge. Creative marketing and promotions must make good in three specific areas.

First, amid the clutter of promotions, advertising, news and communication in general, creative marketing *must* work its way through to capture the attention of consumers.

Second, borrowed interest has been put aside, replaced by the demand for promotions that build the brand. Whether it's imagery, information, or simple purchase habits and usage, promotion has been moved very close to the world of advertising in the demand that it help build brands.

Third, promoters must cut costs. This is no surprise. Simply, achieve the first two directives with less money than you've had before. Make your money work harder to build brands stronger and more profitably in a tougher marketplace that's more cluttered with other messages than ever before.

Creatively, what do these directives mean? Realistically, we'll still see a lot of the same old stuff—borrowed interest Super Bowl promotions that keep talking to the trade and ongoing Kraft Salad Day storewide-type promotions for the brands that have enough clout to keep them in-store. But we'll also see more tie-ins with other manufacturers, retailers and service organizations as marketers try to stretch dollars. And hopefully these tie-ins will start to make more sense as tie-in partners more closely examine the fit for image and promotion potential.

Executionally, we see a trend emerging of "non-creative"

EXHIBIT 5.17 Promotion testing that measures effectiveness based on "stop ability," recall, value, and intent-to-use started the onslaught of "non-creative promotional" ads in FSIs. Reprinted with permission.

EXHIBIT 5.18 Pillsbury made a real event out of Doughboy's 25th Birthday, building the value of the Pillsbury brand name with every candle added to the cake. Totally integrated television, print, display, and even Doughboy's own cookbook magazine supported the event. Reprinted with permission.

ads—simplified layouts, copy, and tactics in promotional media. Packaged goods manufacturers are leading this trend, bolstered by FSI research that shows simple page ads that shout savings and show the product big are winning in the "attention" and "intent to clip" standings. (See Exhibit 5.17.)

On a much more positive note, there has been an equally strong rush of truly creative promotions hitting our mailboxes and store shelves. The in-ad premiums lead the way—the pop-out champagne cork from Salem, the pop-up TransAmerica Building, the do-it-yourself ad from Absolut, L'Oreal's on-page eye shadow samples, and the barrage of interesting Christmas tags, stickers, and holograms from the liquor companies.

Big events like the Bud Bowl and the Pillsbury Doughboy's 25th Birthday (shouldn't he be called the "Doughman" by now?) show that marketers are bringing together all the marketing elements—advertising, display, trade programs, even packaging—to promote a real brand event and get much more for their money than from borrowed interest or coupon drop promotions. (See Exhibit 5.18.)

As promotional marketers faced with creative issues every day, we often become jaded and sometimes review our work wondering if our audience has tired of our games and ploys. Clearly, the state lotteries have raised the ante for sweepstakes grand prizes. And postage stamp costs have sent "quarter back refunds" the way of jingle contests. Yet every time McDonald's introduces a new game or we see a really great premium like Green Giant's Little Sprout bank, and we see consumers getting as excited as we are, we're inspired to keep pushing a little harder and keep stretching our imaginations one more step to make even a coupon drop a creative brand-building exercise.

Where to Get New Ideas

Sales promotion is essentially a creative business, built totally on good ideas. A lot of solid marketing knowledge needs to be behind these ideas, but without one, you don't have a promotion.

Before I reveal my hiding places for good ideas, there are two important points you need to remember:

First, you have to keep alert to good ideas; they will not come out to find you. When I read, I keep one eye on content and story, while the other eye is looking for ideas. I think of ways in which any of my clients or potential clients could benefit from what I see.

Second, do something with the idea, don't just think about it. Tell it to someone who could make it bigger; sell it to someone; expose it to others for feedback—but do something with it!

Now, here are a few places where you can look for good sales promotion ideas:

- *USA Today*—my favorite fast and inexpensive read on what America is interested in today. I've never picked up an issue without finding at least three thought starters. Look for *who* is new, *what* people are doing, and *how* they're doing it.
- *Travelling*—keep your eyes open at airports, hotels, ticket counters. Check out every offer and brochure—there may be one with the solution to your marketing problem on it. Also look at the people. Travellers are often heavy users of many products and have some very ingenious ways to cope with different situations. Maybe you'll see an answer out there.
- *Your own mail box*—start looking at the stuff you've been throwing out.
- *Stores*—go wherever your product is sold and look for ideas in any stores you admire in general. Shop for ideas that retailers could use, for line extension ideas, for tie-in partners, for new services your client could offer. For cutting-edge ideas, check out new video stores.
- *Your service or product*—what could you add, alter, or subtract to make a marketing difference?
- *Other products or services*—some of the companies to watch for good fresh thinking are Kraft General Foods, Absolut Vodka, Apple Computer, Budweiser, and fast food restaurants.

- *Magazines*—see what's hot with the younger set with *Sassy* and *Rolling Stone*. Then check out some of the terrific new "senior" publications like *Lear's*. Get a pulse on what America is thinking, group by group.
- *Your target audience*—spend an evening or two in focus groups and just listen for ideas.
- *Old ideas or borrowed ideas*—look through the old best promotions books and awards. What was a winner in 1979 in another category could be just the idea you need today. Look through old files, think about current promotions you admire, and see if they can be reworked to apply to your situation.
- *Walking your dog*—no matter how many places you look and how many different ways you've thought of to find the big idea, sometimes it just takes a quiet walk around the block to let the good ideas rise to the top.

That's where I get my ideas. There are plenty of new ones in each of these secret places, so join me in the search.

Share Wars of Our Own

The '90s are going to be a tough place to do business for promotion agencies. I saw it coming in 1987 when I heard Burnett had hired Jerry Reitman, a terrific direct marketer, to head up the new Burnett service. They were the last big agency hold out, the last advertising agency to give lip service to, but not make a capital investment in, the people behind true direct marketing and promotion capabilities.

Once Burnett made the commitment, it was as if share wars were formalized. Burnett, like other advertising agencies, was not as concerned about capturing the inflated dollar expenditures the media were saying were being spent on sales promotion. Most of those dollars were going for trade deals and not into anyone else's pockets. What Burnett and other agencies were buying into was the ability to talk about promotion and direct their clients on the subject—to *protect* images and strategies they had helped develop over the years.

The sheer number of promotional marketing agencies has grown substantially throughout the '80s, as marketers in all industries looked for expertise in the field. And now it's time for the shake out. Though it was taboo in the business for years, we're beginning to see more ''sampling'' in the form of spec work. There are discounts or creative financial arrangements, competitive bidding, and rebates (or kickbacks in some circles). We're getting ourselves into the same situation that we've been counseling our clients against.

The ad agencies have completed their buying sprees of promotion agencies and now will either figure out how to make money with them, will keep them for control and client service, or will give up and divest themselves of these different businesses. The fall of FKB in England in 1990 is a somewhat exaggerated example of agencies miscalculating the profitability of acquiring ''below the line'' businesses. They tested the waters of bringing together similar but different businesses and, profit and energy-wise, realized too late that their acquisitions were not fully grounded.

Other agencies will continue to ''orchestrate''/offer the ''whole egg''/ or integrate marketing communications. But only when this integration actually finds its way back to the client's business, will it be a viable marriage. And most agencies haven't the management, the direction, or the systems in place to deliver synergy to their clients. At some point, clients and agency upper management will decide whether ''below the line'' services truly contribute or whether they only are a distraction.

While advertising agencies may be in a position to float and subsidize their new promotion partners as they begin to work together, at some point, the promotion guys need to ''make their numbers.'' Even more critical, the independent promotion agencies themselves must learn how to make money again in this changing climate.

So Now What?

The answers for the '90s are the same ones that have been in marketing books and journals for years. The agencies that will remain strong are those that clearly have a plan and can deliver added value to their clients. Today, you need a position, a unique selling proposition, to stand out from the rest. Will you compete using creativity and quality execution as your strengths? Will you offer flawless full service capabilities? A unique knowledge of a trade class or new product introduction success? You need a way to stand out and then you need to deliver on it.

Our product, the widgets we make, are our promotions and our thinking. The quality of our inventory is reflected daily by the quality of people walking into our offices each day. So finding, hiring, and training the best will help keep our products strong.

Self-promotion, which we all too often forget about, will be even more important, whether it's through winning awards, getting valuable trade press, or doing our own marketing. And, of course, the pricing and profits should be reviewed and adjusted frequently, not just for growth but for stability in this unsettling environment.

Most importantly, we need to add value to our clients business. If you're in a promotion agency and it seems as if you're getting the "vendor treatment" rather than being a partner in your clients' business, ask yourself, "what have I done today to make my client's business better?" What can you do to add value to the relationship so that your agency is not a commodity but a brand name product that represents a good value and fulfills a need. What can you do that cements that loyalty?

Finally, we can expect to see some promotion agencies fold, whether they just close their doors or whether they are shut by advertising agencies, or merged with the other shops for profitability reasons. Spending levels in America are really leveling off and where growth in the '80s came from new industries and divestitures, we can't depend on anything like this in the future. If the recession continues, which traditionally has meant more promotion action, corporate America is likely to be under different marching orders for this slump. Where marketers had the go-ahead to spend for short-term gains, this time Wall Street and boards of directors have passed on the charge to control costs for profitability—*not* to spend more. So the push is on for more effective use of marketing dollars, more bang for the buck.

Our business in the '90s is a lot like our clients' businesses. And we must ask ourselves the same questions that we ask our clients. We need to look at our industry as we would any other in a share war. And use our very best thinking to deliver an agency recommendation that will lead us soundly and successfully into the 21st century.

Index